MEDICAL LAW

Jonathan Herring

PEARSON

Longman

Harlow, England • London • New York • Boston • San Francisco • Toronto • Sydney • Singapore • Hong Kong
Tokyo • Seoul • Taipei • New Delhi • Cape Town • Madrid • Mexico City • Amsterdam • Munich • Paris • Milan

Pearson Education Limited
Edinburgh Gate
Harlow
Essex CM20 2JE
England

and Associated Companies throughout the world

Visit us on the World Wide Web at:
www.pearsoned.co.uk

First published 2008
Revised edition published 2009

© Pearson Education Limited 2008, 2009

ISBN: 978-1-4058-7428-1

British Library Cataloguing-in-Publication Data
A catalogue record for this book is available from the British Library

Library of Congress Cataloging-in-Publication Data
A catalog record for this book is available from the Library of Congress

10 9 8 7 6 5 4 3 2 1
12 11 10 09 08

Typeset by 3 in 10pt Helvetica Condensed
Printed in Great Britain by Henry Ling Ltd., at the Dorset Press, Dorchester, Dorset

The publisher's policy is to use paper manufactured from sustainable forests.

Contents

Supporting resources

Visit the *Law Express Series* Companion Website at **www.pearsoned.co.uk/lawexpress** to find valuable student learning material.

Companion Website for students

▉ A study plan test to assess how well you know the subject before you begin your revision, now broken down into targeted study units

▉ Interactive quizzes with a variety of question types to test your knowledge of the main points from each chapter of the book

▉ Further examination questions and guidelines for answering them

▉ Interactive flashcards to help you revise the main terms and cases

▉ Printable versions of the topic maps and checklists

▉ 'You be the marker' allows you to see exam questions and answers from the perspective of the examiner and includes notes on how an answer might be marked

▉ Podcasts provide point-by-point instruction on how to answer a common exam question

Also: The Companion Website provides the following features:

▉ Search tool to help locate specific items of content

▉ E-mail results and profile tools to send results of quizzes to instructors

▉ Online help and support to assist with website usage and troubleshooting

For more information please contact your local Pearson Education sales representative or visit **www.pearsoned.co.uk/lawexpress**

Acknowledgements

I am grateful to all those at Pearson Education who work on this series. In particular, Rebekah Taylor, who has provided invaluable guidance on the format and flavour of the books. I am also very grateful to my wife Kirsten and daughters Laurel, Jo and Darcy for all their love, support and distraction during the writing of this book.

Jonathan Herring
July 2007

■Publisher's acknowledgements

Our thanks go to all reviewers who contributed to the development of this text, including students who participated in research and focus groups which helped to shape the series format.

Introduction

Medical law is a fascinating subject. It raises all kinds of interesting debates and different clashes of principle. It is certainly a topic on which people tend to have very strong views. In fact, beware, you can lose friends if you get too heated discussing these ethical principles! But listening to others in a respectful way can teach you about a variety of different ways of understanding the world, our bodies and the power of medicine.

Because it can be such a controversial area, students can get carried away when writing exams. There are three dangers, in particular. First, in the exam hall, do not write a rant instead of an essay. Remember, you do not know what view the person marking the exam will take and so it is dangerous to be too rude about views you disagree with. However strong your views, you should consider the variety of views on a topic in a sensitive way. This is not to say that your essay should simply summarise the views of others and not make clear your own view. Many essay questions will ask you to set out your views on a controversial issue. But in doing so you can explain the views of others and why you do not find them convincing. Second, it is easy to end up writing an essay which fails to mention any law at all. As you will be taking a law exam, this is not a very good idea! So make sure wherever possible that you are referring to relevant statutory provision or case law. Even if your essay question is more theoretical, show how theoretical debates become relevant in particular cases. Third, there is a danger in polarising debates into two extreme positions, whereas, in fact, there may be several compromise views available. Abortion is an area where the debate often breaks down into two camps: pro-life or pro-choice. There are, however, middle positions between these two views. That said, you may well conclude that such compromise positions are 'messy' and indicate indecisiveness and a failure to deal with the issues. Still, beware of presenting ethical debates as simply a choice between two extreme views.

There are a number of themes which run across the different topics covered in this book and in most medical law courses. For example, the extent to which patients have the right to decide whether or not to receive treatment; the moral and legal status of the embryo; the extent to which patients have rights and responsibilities. These issues raise their heads at a number of places in a medical law course. In an essay question in an exam, it can be interesting to demonstrate how an issue which is raised in one topic reflects debates that appear in other subjects. In other words, don't see medical law as being made up of a number of discrete boxes which have nothing to do with each other. Rather it involves the balancing of different principles and values in a variety of different contexts.

The primary aim of this book is to help you to revise for your exams. To be honest, if so far you have done no work, attended no lectures, and read no other material, you will get little help from this book. If, however, you have been doing some work but are feeling overwhelmed by the amount of material available and are unsure how to put it together in order to revise for the exam, this is the book for you. A first-class answer is likely to include references to more cases than are found in this book and will discuss more theoretical issues than are discussed here. What this book can do is to set you off on the right step for your revision. It will help you see the wood for the trees and emphasise the points that you *must* know. Hopefully, most of the material in this book you will have come across before, but it will help put it in some kind of order and help you see how it can be used to answer questions in the exam. If you have read and understood this book, you will have at your fingertips the key cases and principles to do well in the exam.

REVISION NOTES

▮ Don't forget to include plenty of law in your answers.
▮ Show the examiner that you are aware of a variety of different ethical approaches to the issues.
▮ Be respectful of the views of others, even when you violently disagree with them.

Guided tour

Topic maps – Highlight the main points and allow you to find your way quickly and easily through each chapter.

Revision checklist – How well do you know each topic? Don't panic if you don't know them all, the chapters will help you revise each point so that you will be fully prepared for your exams.

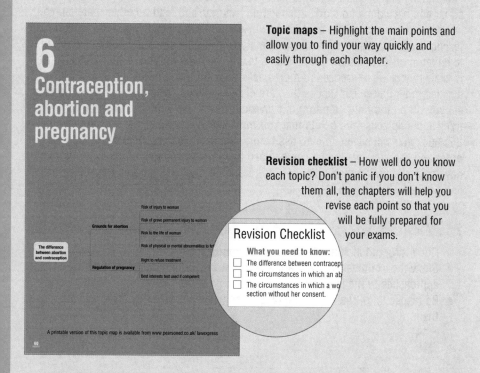

6
Contraception, abortion and pregnancy

Risk of injury to woman

Risk of grave permanent injury to woman

Grounds for abortion

Risk to the life of woman

Risk of physical or mental abnormalities to fet

Right to refuse treatment

Regulation of pregnancy

Best interests test used if competent

The difference between abortion and contraception

A printable version of this topic map is available from www.pearsoned.co.uk/ lawexpress

Revision Checklist

What you need to know:

☐ The difference between contracep

☐ The circumstances in which an ab

☐ The circumstances in which a wo
    section without her consent.

Sample questions – Prepare for what you will be faced with in your exams! Guidance on structuring strong answers is provided at the end of the chapter.

Sample question

Could you answer this question? Below is a typical problem question that could arise on this topic. Guidelines on answering the question are included at the end of this chapter, whilst a sample essay question and guidance on tackling it can be found on the Companion Website.

Problem question

Adam and Eve are an unmarried couple who have had trouble conceiving a child. They approach a licensed clinic for treatment. They are offered treatment using donated sperm, from Dave, and a donated egg from Mary. During the weeks they are receiving information and tests, Adam and Eve's relationship comes to an end. However, they

---

Key definition boxes – Make sure you understand essential legal terms.

KEY DEFINITION

Murder. A person is guilty of murder if he or she:

▪ caused the death of the victim
▪ intended to cause death or grievous bodily harm
▪ cannot successfully raise a defence.

Problem area boxes – Highlight areas where students most often trip up in exams. Use them to make sure you do not make the same mistakes.

> **Problem area:** What happens if section 1 is breached?
>
> Although section 1 makes it clear what medical professionals must do if they are to act lawfully, the statute does not make it clear what the legal consequences are if a professional does not meet the requirements in section 1. It may be that an offence of theft will be committed or perhaps a tortious wrong.

Key case and key statute boxes – Identify the essential cases and statutes that you need to know for your exams.

> **KEY CASE**
>
> *MH* v. *Secretary of State for*
>
> Concerning: whether section 2
>
> **Facts**
>
> M was a severely mentally disabled of the Mental Health Act 1983. Un to the Mental Health Review Tribu incapable of doing this and there to be appointed a guardian wa way section 2 placed the bu interfered with her righte

> **KEY STATUTE**
>
> **Mental Health Act, section 3(2)**
>
> 'An application for admission for treatment may be m patient on the grounds that –
>
> (a) he is suffering from a mental disorder of a na makes it appropriate for him to receive medical t and
>
> (b) it is necessary for the health or safety of the protection of other persons that he should receiv

Further thinking boxes – Illustrate areas of academic debate, and point you towards that extra reading required for the top grades.

> **FURTHER THINKING**
>
> Why does it matter when death occurs? If a person is about to die anyway, what is so very wrong in removing their organs shortly before death? Is it possible to define death or is it better to see death as a process (see Chau and Herring (2007))? Some critics of brain-stem death claim this elevates the brain to being the only organ of significance in the body. If a person's heart is still beating and their body is still working, should the fact that their brain has ceased to function be of any relevance?

Glossary – Forgotten the meaning of a word? Where a word is highlighted in the text, turn to the glossary at the back of the book to remind yourself of its meaning.

Glossary of terms

The glossary is divided into two parts: **key definitions** and **other useful terms**.

The **key definitions** can be found within relevant chapters as well as at the end of the book. These are the essential terms that you must know and understand in order to prepare for an examination or a piece of coursework.

The **other useful terms** provide definitions of other terms and phrases which you will encounter in this subject and may have forgotten the meaning of. These terms are highlighted in the text as they occur but the definition can only be found here.

Key definitions

Advance decision	An advance decision is a decision by a patient made about the treatment he/she wished to receive, or not to receive, if he/she lost capacity. It must have been made when the patient was over 18 and had capacity. The advance decision only becomes effective when the patient loses capacity
Consequentialism	This approach decides whether an act is ethically right or wrong by looking at its consequences. Quite simply, if it

Exam tips – Want to impress examiners? These indicate how you can improve your exam performance and your chances of getting top marks.

> **EXAM TIP**
>
> The issue of the anonymity of donors is a controversial one and it is worth revising the issue carefully. Consider the different human rights that could be claimed here? How important is a child's right to know their genetic origins? Is such a right enforceable if (as the evidence suggests) parents are unwilling to tell their children that they were born using donor sperm? If the sperm-donor shortage continues, should donor anonymity be restored?

Revision notes – Highlight points that you should be aware of in other topic areas, or where your course may adopt a specific approach that you should check with your course tutor before reading further.

> **REVISION NOTE**
>
> In reaching the decision in *Axon*, the judge placed a lot of weight on the decision of the House of Lords in *Gillick* v. *West Norfolk and Wisbech*, discussed in Chapter 3. Although from the discussion of the law on children and consent generally, in theory at least, even if a child did not want to have an abortion, a doctor could rely on the consent of her parent in order to give her one.

Guided tour of the companion website

 Book resources are available to download. Print your own **topic maps** and **revision checklists!**

 Use the **study plan** prior to your revision to help you assess how well you know the subject and determine which areas need most attention. Choose to take the full assessment or focus on targeted study units.

 'Test your knowledge' of individual areas with quizzes tailored specifically to each chapter. A variety of multiple choice, true and false and fill-in-the-blank question types ensure you are prepared for anything. Sample problem and essay questions are also available with guidance on crafting a good answer.

 Flashcards help improve recall of important legal terms and key cases. Use online, print for a handy reference or download to iPod for on-the-go revision!

'You be the marker' gives you the chance to evaluate sample exam answers for different question types and understand how and why an examiner awards marks.

Download the **podcast** and listen as your own personal Law Express tutor guides you through a 10-15 minute audio session. You will be presented with a typical but challenging question and provided a step-by-step explanation on how to approach the question, what essential elements your answer will need for a pass, how to structure a good response, and what to do to make your answer stand out so that you can earn extra marks.

All of this and more can be found when you visit **www.pearsoned.co.uk/lawexpress**

Table of cases and statutes

■ Cases

■ Statutes

Statutory instruments

European and international legislation

1

Basic principles of medical law and ethics

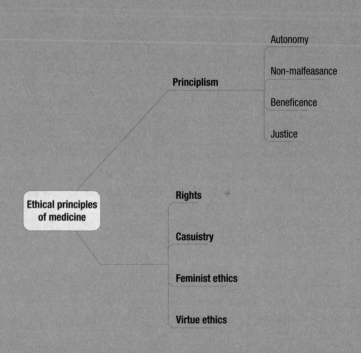

- Principlism
  - Autonomy
  - Non-malfeasance
  - Beneficence
  - Justice
- Ethical principles of medicine
  - Rights
  - Casuistry
  - Feminist ethics
  - Virtue ethics

A printable version of this topic map is available from www.pearsoned.co.uk/lawexpress

Revision Checklist

What you need to know:

- [ ] Some of the key approaches to medical ethics
- [ ] The key legal principles governing medical law
- [ ] How ethical principles and medical principles interrelate.

Introduction

'Doctor knows best.'

This used to be a governing principle in medical law. But nowadays there is much talk of the rights of patients and the responsibilities of doctors. What has not changed are the heated debates over the complex ethical issues that medicine raises. Some medical ethicists have produced a series of principles which they suggest can be applied to provide guidance in difficult cases. Other ethicists are less convinced that general rules can be developed and that it is better to fashion results that are right for individual cases. Although the law is influenced by ethical principles, it does not follow that the law and ethics match. It is unlikely that the law would require a medical professional to act in an unethical way. On the other hand, it cannot be assumed that just because something is legal it is also ethical.

Essay question advice
An essay question is likely to ask you to assess some of the leading ethical principles. You will need to describe them and give examples of how they are reflected in legal principles. You may also need to consider whether there are problems with the principles and the clashes that arise between them. For example, should autonomy be regarded as an overarching principle? There is also the debate over whether it is desirable to have general principles that are applied, or whether it is preferable to treat each case individually. An essay question might require you to consider how the law interacts with the different ethical principles. Should legal responses always match the ethical ones? Good answers will show how the disputes over these general principles are reflected in real cases, using examples from the case law.

Sample question

Could you answer this question? Below is a typical essay question that could arise on this topic. Guidelines on answering the question are included at the end of this chapter.

Essay question

Is it useful to develop key ethical principles governing medical issues? Is it possible to develop an effective way of reconciling clashes between these principles?

■ Consequentialism and deontology

Don't be frightened by these long words; the basic concepts behind them are not too difficult to grasp.

KEY DEFINITION

Consequentialism. This approach decides whether an act is ethically right or wrong by looking at its consequences. Quite simply, if it produces more good than bad, the act is ethically right.

KEY DEFINITION

Deontology. This approach says that it is right or wrong to infringe certain principles, regardless of the consequences. For example, some people believe it is never right to intentionally kill another person, however much good may be produced as a result.

A good example of where these two approaches might produce a different result is this. A doctor finds out that his patient is HIV positive. The patient refuses to tell his wife and intends to carry on having sexual relations with her. Should the doctor tell the wife about the husband's condition? A consequentialist may well answer 'yes'. The benefit of this will be that it will protect the wife from infection. Although the patient may be distressed, this will be less harm than that suffered by the wife. A deontologist may say there is an absolute principle that doctors must respect their patients' confidentiality. This principle should not be broken, just because it will produce more good than harm.

Using the example just given, we can see that actually the distinction between consequentialism and deontology is not as clear-cut as may, at first, be thought. For a consequentialist, are we to take into account that if the doctor tells the wife, patients as a group may start to trust their doctors less? This may have seriously bad consequences. Indeed, if a doctor breaches a moral principle (even if it produces a good result), this may lead to a loss in trust in the medical profession and so produce harmful results. This may mean that there is less difference between the approaches than may be thought. And might not the deontologist say that the governing principle is that, unless very serious harm will otherwise result, a confidence should be respected? This will lead to a position closer to that taken by the consequentialist.

■Four key ethical principles

In a highly influential book Tom Beauchamp and James Childress (2001) have suggested four principles which they say are a 'common morality'. In other words, they are principles which all societies should be able to accept. Their four principles are:

- respect for autonomy
- non-malfeasance
- beneficence
- justice.

Autonomy

Many ethicists believe that autonomy is the most important of all principles for medical ethics. It states that patients have the right to make decisions over what medical treatment they should receive. It is never permissible for a doctor to give a patient treatment without the patient's consent, unless the patient is incompetent, or maybe that is necessary to avoid serious harm to others. Even if the decision of the patient not to receive the treatment seems perverse or foolish, it must be respected (see Chapter 3 for further discussion).

Note, however, that respect of autonomy does not mean that patients have the right to demand treatment that they want. The law strongly respects the right of a patient to say 'no' (see Chapter 3), but not the right to demand treatment by saying 'yes' (see Chapter 2). The NHS could not afford to give patients every treatment they wanted.

An example of the principle of autonomy in practice is the following:

KEY CASE

St George's Healthcare NHS Trust v. *S* [1998] 3 All ER 673

Concerning: whether it was lawful to perform a Caesarean section operation on a woman without her consent

Facts

S was 35 weeks pregnant when she was told she needed to have a Caesarean section operation. She was told that without one she and/or the fetus would die. She refused to consent. Her doctors assessed her competent to make the decision to refuse, but sought judicial approval to perform the operation. This was given by Hogg J, and a baby girl was born as a result. After the birth, the mother appealed against Hogg J's decision.

Legal principle

The Court of Appeal held that the mother's detention and the performance of the operation without her consent was unlawful. They confirmed that if a competent woman had an absolute right to refuse treatment, this was not affected by the fact she was pregnant. If a competent pregnant woman refuses to consent to medical intervention, it cannot be imposed upon her. This is so even if without it she and the fetus will die.

REVISION NOTE

The principle of autonomy is particularly important when considering for the legal requirement that a patient gives consent to treatment. This is discussed in Chapter 3. You will see there that the law now strongly protects the right of a patient to refuse treatment.

FURTHER THINKING

It should not be thought that the principle of autonomy is without its critics, at least as an absolute principle. Should a patient be permitted to refuse to consent to treatment even if this will mean that a huge burden will be placed on the patient's family to care for him or her? (See Herring (2007).) Do patients not have responsibilities as well as rights? (See Brazier (2006).) Further, is it right that patients should be able to refuse treatment if this will leave them in an . undignified and distressing state? For example, should a patient be able to refuse to be washed while in hospital?

The principle of non-malfeasance

This principle is straightforward. Doctors must not harm their patients. At first it might be thought to be so obvious as to not need stating. However, it should be recalled that there can be a temptation in some cases to harm one patient in order to benefit another (e.g. by taking tissue for a transplant). This principle would not permit that. Some commentators argue that whether a procedure harms a patient depends on the patient's point of view. If a patient consents to the taking of an organ for transplantation, then it cannot be said to constitute harm. There is much to be said for that, but then it becomes hard to distinguish the non-malfeasance principle from the autonomy principle.

The following case demonstrates that it can be difficult sometimes to know whether a procedure will harm a patient.

KEY CASE

Simms v. *Simms* [2003] 1 All ER 669

Concerning: when experimental surgery was lawful

Facts

Two teenagers were suffering from variety Creutzfeldt-Jakob Disease. Their doctors proposed a novel treatment which had not been tested on humans. The expert evidence suggested that the effectiveness of the surgery was unknown. Without the treatment, the individuals would die. Their parents sought a declaration that it was lawful for the proposed treatment to be given.

Legal principle

Butler Sloss P authorised the surgery. As the two teenagers were incompetent to make the decision, the question was simply whether doing the surgery would be in their best interests. She held that it was. Although medical opinion was divided on whether or not the treatment would be given, the experts agreed it would not be irresponsible to give the treatment. The chance of success might be slight, but given they were facing death, it was a risk worth taking. She attached 'considerable weight' to the fact that the parents supported using the treatment.

The principle of beneficence

KEY DEFINITION

Principle of beneficence. Medical professionals must provide the best medical treatment for their patients.

In the current climate this is a problematic principle. The best treatment may be too expensive for the NHS to provide. See the discussion of rationing in Chapter 2. Further, commentators add that this principle must be seen in conjunction with the principle of autonomy. Medical professionals cannot give a patient the best treatment against the wishes of the patient and then seek to rely on the principle of beneficence.

EXAM TIP

Although the principle of beneficence sounds straightforward, it does raise some interesting issues. Should patients who want to be given treatment which is not in their best interests, but who are willing to pay for it, be denied the treatment? For example, should there be much greater restrictions on cosmetic surgery? What if a patient objects on religious grounds to a proposed treatment and wants a far less effective alternative?

The principle of justice

KEY DEFINITION

The **principle of justice.** Patients should be treated equally and fairly. One patient should not be improperly given preferential treatment over others.

While most people will agree that patients should be treated justly, there is much dispute over quite what this means. The dispute mostly comes to the fore in cases of rationing, which we shall look at in Chapter 2. If a young patient is given an expensive treatment, but an older patient suffering from the same medical condition is not, is this an infringement of the principle of justice?

EXAM TIP

Gillon (2003) provides a good summary of these principles. Note that he thinks that autonomy should be regarded as the most important principle. Some people are concerned that if whenever there is a clash between autonomy and the other principles, autonomy wins out, then, in effect, there is only one principle (namely autonomy) and not four.

▶

■Rights

The notion of rights in the medical arenas has been of growing importance for ethicists and lawyers, for lawyers, in particular, because of the Human Rights Act 1998.

KEY DEFINITION

The concept of a right in law is much disputed and it is not possible to give a definition which would be accepted by everyone. When a person has a right to x, other people are bound by a duty to protect or promote the interests the person has in x. There need to be good reasons why the person should be prevented from x.

Some of the most important rights that can be found in the European Convention on Human Rights (ECHR) for medical lawyers include the following:

Right in the European Convention	Legal Principle
Article 2: the right to life	A doctor may not intentionally kill a patient (see Chapter 9)
Article 3: the right to protection from torture, inhuman or degrading treatment	A doctor must not, where possible, leave a patient in a state which is inhuman or degrading
Article 8: the right to respect of private life	A patient has an absolute right to refuse treatment (see Chapter 3)
Article 8: the right to respect of family life	A doctor should consult with parents, where possible, before providing treatment to children (unless the child is sufficiently mature to make his or her own decision)
Article 14: the right not to be discriminated against	A doctor may not allocate health-care resources based on age or sex

■ Casuistry

Casuistry emphasises that each case is different. It argues that rather that seeking to develop grand principles that apply across the board, each should be treated on its own. It is more effective to compare and contrast a case with similar ones, rather than seeking to apply a meta-principle. The difficulty with such an approach is that it might be harder for doctors or other health professionals to determine what is ethically the correct approach if there are no general 'rules' to apply.

■ Virtue ethics

Virtue ethicists emphasise that people should do the right thing and for the right reasons. A common way of approaching an issue is therefore to ask what character is manifested by a person acting in this way for this reason. So, for example, using a virtue ethics approach Hursthouse (1991) suggests that a woman who decides to have an abortion so that her holiday plans are not interfered with is not acting in a good way. Whereas a woman who had an abortion because she believed that the life of the child born would be intolerable, would be acting in a virtuous way. Note that this would be so even if the woman's decision was based on a mistaken diagnosis by a doctor. Her character revealed by her act would be good (arguably), even if in fact the act did not produce a good (arguably).

■ Feminist medical ethics

Feminist ethics emphasises that it is not possible to understand medical law and how it operates in practice without appreciating how it operates in a world of gender inequality. Feminist approaches have demonstrated how medicine and medical law has been used as a way of exercising power over women (e.g. through controlling them during pregnancy). Many feminist writers have also promoted the use of an ethic of care.

KEY DEFINITION

Ethic of care. This is an ethical approach which emphasises that we all live in relationship with other people and are dependent upon other people. It is, therefore, not possible to look at a patient and ask what rights he or she has as a lone individual or what is best for the patient. Rather we need to ask what is best for this group of people who are in relationship together. It values interdependency and mutuality over individual freedom.

Problem area: The dangers of an ethic of care

Initially, an ethic of care sounds very attractive. There are good arguments to be used in favour of taking account of the interests of carers when making medical decisions (see Herring (2007)). However, we also know that those who are meant to be caring for relatives do abuse them. There is a danger that relatives can manipulate the notion of ethic of care to take advantage of older people.

Religious perspectives

Historically, and for many people still today, religious arguments have played an important role in deciding issues of medical ethics. It is notable that most religious views indicate a clear answer: an activity either is or is not permissible in God's eyes. Many writing from a non-religious perspective are far less sure there is a 'right answer' and tend to be more willing to allow practices if those involved consent.

Chapter Summary:
Putting it all together

TEST YOURSELF

- [ ] Can you tick all the points from the revision checklist at the beginning of this chapter?
- [ ] Take the **end-of-chapter quiz** on the Companion Website.
- [ ] Test your knowledge of the cases below with the **revision flashcards** on the website.
- [ ] Attempt the essay question from the beginning of the chapter using the guidelines below.
- [ ] Go to the Companion Website to try out other questions.

Answer guidelines

See the essay question at the start of the chapter.

A useful starting point in answering this question would be to go through the four key principles that Beauchamp and Childress (2001) have developed (as summarised above). You could then discuss whether these principles are useful. Do you agree that each case involves individuals and is different, and that it is not always possible to generate overarching principles that take account of all the different circumstances?

Or is it useful for doctors to have general principles to apply so that they do not get caught up in the emotional and personal issues that are raised?

You can then turn to consider how clashes between these principles should be resolved. Do you think that autonomy should be the paramount principle? Are there any circumstances in which you think it appropriate to give a patient treatment against his or her wishes? Or where it is inappropriate, to give a treatment that a patient wishes to receive?

FURTHER READING

Beauchamp, T. and Childress, J. (2001) *Principles of Biomedical Ethics*. Oxford: OUP.

Brazier, M. (2006) 'Do no Harm – Do Patients Have Responsibilities Too?', 65 *Cambridge Law Journal* 397.

Gillon, R. (2003) 'Ethics Needs Principles – Four Can Encompass the Rest – and Respect for Autonomy Should Be "First among Equals" ' 29 *Journal of Medical Ethics* 307.

Harris, J. (ed.) (2001) *Bioethics*. Oxford: OUP.

Harris, J. (2003) 'In Praise of Unprincipled Ethics', 29 *Journal of Medial Ethics* 303.

Herring, J. (2007) 'Where Are the Carers in Healthcare Law and Ethics?', 27 *Legal Studies* 51.

Hope, T. (2005) *A Very Short Introduction to Medical Ethics*. Oxford: OUP.

Hursthouse, R. (1991) 'Virtue Theory and Abortion', 20 *Philosophy and Public Affairs* 223.

Kuhse, H. and Singer, P. (eds) (1998) *A Companion to Bioethics*. Oxford: Blackwell.

2
Rationing

Rationing of medical resources → The role of NICE

- Successful judicial challenges
- Unsucessful judicial challenges
- The impact of European law
- Ethical issues raised

A printable version of this topic map is available from www.pearsoned.co.uk/lawexpress

Revision Checklist

What you need to know:

- [ ] What rationing is
- [ ] How rationing decisions are made in the NHS
- [ ] How a rationing decision can be challenged in the courts
- [ ] The attitude of the courts towards rationing decisions.
- [ ] The ethical issues surrounding rationing decisions.

Introduction

In an ideal world everyone would get the medical treatment they need.

However, it is generally agreed this is not possible, at least not without taxation at a higher level than it is currently. It would be simply too expensive to fund the treatment that everyone would like. Rationing decisions, therefore, need to be made to decide who will receive the limited resources available. In some cases rationing is not due to a lack of money, but a lack of other medical resources. An example is organ donation where there is a finite number of organs available for transplantation and simply not enough for everyone's need. The question of how to decide which treatments are available on the NHS and how to select which treatments a patient should receive is a highly controversial question. Not surprisingly, the courts, in recent years, have been drawn into the debates with legal challenges being brought over rationing decisions.

Essay question advice

In an essay question you will need a good knowledge of the cases where rationing decisions have been challenged. There have not been too many of them and so you can be expected to know them well. You will need to discuss the work of the National Institute of Clinical Excellence (NICE). You should also address some of the issues which academics have debated: should age be relevant in rationing decisions?; should it be relevant that patients have brought their condition upon themselves?; how are we to assess who is in greatest need?

A problem question is likely to ask you to consider what legal challenges could be made to a rationing decision. The case law will need to be used carefully in addressing the question. Note that although several challenges have been successful, the courts are still generally reluctant to allow legal challenges. Anyone seeking to challenge a rationing decision will face an uphill battle. Do not exaggerate the significance of the cases and note how the judges have been careful to limit the impact of their decisions. A good answer will also raise the possible significance of the Human Rights Act to these decisions.

Sample question

Could you answer this question? Below is a typical problem question that could arise on this topic. Guidelines on answering the question are included at the end of this chapter, whilst a sample problem question and guidance on tackling it can be found on the Companion Website.

Problem question

A new drug has been produced which its makers claim significantly reduces the risk of heart attack in cases of people with high cholesterol. NICE has announced it will be considering the drug in two years' time. Alf, Beatrice, Charlene and Dave have all been denied access to the drug by their local Primary Care Trust (PCT), but for different reasons.

In Alf's case, the PCT says it has a policy of never authorising new drugs until they have been approved by NICE.

In Beatrice's case, the PCT says there is inadequate clinical evidence that the drug is effective.

In Charlene's case, the PCT says it will supply the drug, but only to patients who are caring for children or elderly relatives. Charlene does not fall into this category.

In Dave's case, the PCT has said that it will not fund the drug if a patient's high cholesterol is due to his/her unhealthy diet because patients have only themselves to blame, and it prefers to fund blameless patients. Dave's cholesterol level is blamed on his penchant for eating very fatty foods and so he is denied the drug.

Discuss the chances of Alf, Beatrice, Charlene and Dave in challenging the decisions of their PCTs.

■Rationing

Most people accept that the National Health Service cannot provide every patient with every treatment they may want. There is simply not enough money within the NHS to provide every treatment that is needed. This means decisions have to be made as to which patient can receive which treatment.

KEY DEFINITION

Rationing. Where there is only a limited health-care resource and a decision must be made to offer the resources to some patients and not others.

FURTHER THINKING

Not everyone is convinced that rationing is a necessity. Although funding all treatment that is needed on the NHS would require an increase in taxation (or drastic cuts elsewhere), the increase might not be more than a few percentage points. If politicians were open with the public and said that either life-saving treatments would not be available on the NHS or income tax would have to increase by a few percentage points, are we sure that the public would rather keep low taxes? Indeed, should we simply decide that, morally speaking, society is obliged to provide for the health-care needs of its citizens. If that requires an increase in taxation, that must occur. See Maynard (2001) for further discussion.

It is important to appreciate that rationing can occur at a number of levels within the NHS:

■ The government must decide how much money to allocate to health rather than other needs (e.g. transport).
■ Decisions are made as to how to divide up the health budget among the different bodies and organisations within the NHS.
■ A local body may decide how to allocate its budget to meet the needs of people in its area.
■ A doctor may decide whether or not a particular treatment is cost-effective.

■The role of NICE

The National Institute for Health and Clinical Excellence (NICE) plays an important role in rationing decisions. It has the job of advising on the clinical effectiveness of drugs and their cost effectiveness. Although its guidance is not officially binding on PCTs, it should be followed. Part of the aim in creating NICE was that there would be consistent approaches to controversial treatments across the NHS. This would avoid the so-called 'post code lottery', where patients in some parts of the country have access to treatment, but in other parts do not. In making its decisions, NICE pays much attention to the Quality Adjusted Life Years (QALY) value of treatment.

KEY DEFINITION

Quality adjusted life year. This is an assessment of the benefit of a treatment. It takes into account how many years extra life a treatment may provide and the increase in the quality of life that a treatment may provide.

NICE will consider how many QALYs a treatment will provide and at what cost. This provides a way of comparing treatments for the same medical condition. It also provides a way of comparing treatments for completely different medical conditions. If one treatment offers many years of greatly improved quality of life, it will be preferred over a treatment which will offer only a few years of low quality life. It also enables NICE to consider the costs of different treatments. So a treatment which offers many QALYs at a low price is almost bound to be approved by NICE.

FURTHER THINKING

The use of QALYs is controversial. Is it possible to value quality of life? Is it worse being confined to a wheelchair or being blind? Do we want to start putting figures on such things? Others argue that it works against the interests of older people and those with a disability. This is because they may not be able to show as much gain from the treatment, or for as long a time, as a young person in generally good health. Harris (2005) argues that all patients who require a particular treatment should be entitled to it on the basis of the principle of equality. Further controversy surrounds whether the benefits to those who care for patients should be considered when assessing the gains from the treatment (Herring (2007)), or whether the fact that a patient is at fault in needing the treatment should be relevant (i.e. should we prefer the victim of lung cancer who has endured passive smoke, over the smoker?)

EXAM TIP

In an essay question it is a good idea to discuss the role of NICE. To cynics, NICE was created so that the making of unpalatable decisions on who would or would not receive treatment would be taken by an organisation which is independent of government. In other words, it was a way of deflecting blame away from politicians. Other commentators think that it was sensible to place the decision in an organisation which is free from political pressure and makes decisions which are based on objective facts, rather than which group of patients has the best

▶

pressure group or can garner the most public sympathy. The relationship between NICE and the government has been uneasy, with, in one case, a government minister appearing to overrule a decision by NICE on breast-cancer treatment. There are certainly dangers that, if politicians do start to interfere in decisions made by NICE, the organisation will be more widely seen as a smoke screen. Currently, it appears to have generally a good reputation for making independent judgments. For further discussion, see Syrett (2002).

Judicial challenges to rationing decisions

If a patient wishes to take his or her PCT to court for failing to provide treatment, this is most likely to be done by means of judicial review. It is necessary to show that the decision reached was irrational. Such claims have rarely succeeded because the courts have recognised that health-care bodies often face difficult decisions. The court is not in a position to weigh up all the competing claims that they have on their resources. Although the court will know of the case before it, it will not know the details of all the other cases that the PCT has to deal with. As the following case shows, this point is taken even where the needs of the patient appear compelling.

KEY CASE

R v. *Cambridge HA ex p. B* [1995] 1 WLR 898

Concerning: whether 'life-saving' treatment could be denied

Facts

Jaymee Bowen, aged 10, was suffering from acute myeloid leukaemia. The doctors treating her agreed that the only possible treatment (intense chemotherapy and a bone marrow transplant) was very unlikely to succeed and would be very painful. Her father found a doctor in London who was willing to provide the treatment, but he could not afford the private fees. He sought an order that Cambridge HA pay for the treatment.

Legal principle

The Court of Appeal held that health authorities had to make difficult decisions about how to spend their money. They cannot provide all the treatment they would like. The court cannot require the health authority to justify its resource allocations. In this case the court had to respect the decision of the health authority that this was not treatment which it was appropriate to spend its money on.

Cases where judicial challenges have been successful

Where the health authority has taken a rigid approach which fails to properly take into account each particular individual, this is particularly susceptible to challenge. That is demonstrated by the following cases.

KEY CASE

R v. *North West Lancashire Health Authority, ex p. A* [2000] 1 WLR 977

Concerning: denying gender reassignment surgery

Facts

The applicants suffered gender identity dysphoria. Two of them were found to have a clinical need for gender reassignment surgery (colloquially a 'sex change' operation). The health authority decided that it would not pay for such surgery because it was unclear whether the surgery would be helpful. However, in exceptional cases, the Director of Public Health could authorise funding.

Legal principle

In effect, the policy was a blanket ban on funding the surgery. It was not really imagined that the Director would ever authorise funding in cases of this kind. This meant that individual cases were not considered on their own merits. The approach taken by the HA was, therefore, unlawful. Further, the HA had failed to acknowledge that transsexualism was a medical condition for which the surgery was a recognised treatment.

In the following case it appears to have been the reluctance of the PCT to admit that the decisions were being made on the basis of economics which caused the court problems. A health authority should be open and clear about what its policy is and how it operates. Otherwise, there is a danger it will be successfully challenged in the courts.

KEY CASE

R (Rogers) v. *Swindon NHS Primary Health Care Trust* [2006] EWCA Civ 392

Concerning: rationing drugs for breast cancer

Facts

Swindon Primary Health Care Trust refused to fund Ms Rogers's treatment with Herceptin for breast cancer. Although her consultant had recommended that she use the drug, the PCT had a policy of only funding it in 'exceptional cases' and found that she was not exceptional. She sought judicial review of the PCT's decision

Legal principle

If a PCT decides that monetary issues are not an issue, then all patients who clinically need a particular drug should be given it. There were no clinical or personal reasons that could justify giving the drug to some patients and not others among the group of those for whom the drug was clinically appropriate. A policy of allowing drugs to be given in 'exceptional' cases could only be lawful if it was clear what those exceptional circumstances might be.

EXAM TIP

A good point to make in the exam is that the courts tend to be reluctant to overturn a rationing decision on the basis simply that the decision was wrong. Although it may be willing to do so if the PCT has made an error of fact (e.g. the approach to transsexualism in the *R* v. *NW Lancashire ex p. A* (2000) case), the courts will be more willing to intervene if they are persuaded that the decision-making process is flawed. This might be where a blanket policy is pursued, without considering each case individually, or the real reasons behind a decision not being made open (e.g. where the decision is really made on the basis of financial considerations, but the PCT says it is a clinical decision).

The impact of European Union law

In the following case the potential significance of European Union law was considered. At the heart of the claim is Article 49 of the EC Treaty which allows freedom to provide services within the community. The European Court of Justice has held that services include medical treatment. The question in this case was whether an NHS patient who could not get treatment within a reasonable length of time from the NHS had the right to travel to another EC country for that treatment and then claim recompense from the NHS for the costs.

R (Watts) v. Bedford PCT [2004] EWCA Civ 166

Concerning: whether the NHS could be required to pay for medical treatment received by British citizens in other EU states

Facts

Ms Watts needed a hip transplant. When she was told that this would take over a year under the NHS, she travelled to France and had the operation there. She claimed that under Article 49 of the EC Treaty and Council Regulation 1408/71, Article 22 the NHS had to pay for the treatment.

Legal principle

The English Court of Appeal held that the NHS was not liable to pay. Article 49 did not apply to state-funded health-care systems. Article 22 did not apply where the delay was caused by economic circumstances.

The European Court of Justice disagreed. It held that patients could rely on Article 49 and 22 to claim expenses. In future, where a NHS patient is facing medically unacceptable waiting times, the patient can seek prior authorisation for funding. Any decision will take into account the patient's medical condition and the degree of pain and disability.

The *Watts* decision has been controversial. Supporters say that it means that EU citizens should be entitled to a reasonable standard of health care and that if that cannot be provided in their own country, they must be free to receive it in another country. Opponents are concerned that *Watts* will only help middle-class patients who will have the resources to find hospitals in Europe which can treat them and make the appropriate applications to the PCT. Note there is no requirement on a PCT to find an overseas hospital to provide treatment if its waiting lists become unacceptably long.

Chapter Summary:
Putting it all together

- [ ] Can you tick all the points from the revision checklist at the beginning of this chapter?
- [ ] Take the **end-of-chapter quiz** on the Companion Website.
- [ ] Test your knowledge of the cases below with the **revision flashcards** on the website.
- [ ] Attempt the problem question from the beginning of the chapter using the guidelines below.
- [ ] Go to the Companion Website to try out other questions.

Answer guidelines

See the problem question at the start of the chapter.

You should start by emphasising how hard it is to succeed in challenging a rationing decision. In order to show that the decision has been unreasonable, it has to be shown that the approach taken is so unreasonable that no reasonable health-care body could have made it.

In Alf's case, you will want to make the point that the courts tend to disapprove of strict approaches that fail to take account of each individual case. Notice also that NICE is only meant to offer guidance to a PCT, albeit guidance that it is expected it should follow. A PCT cannot delegate its responsibilities to NICE.

In Beatrice's case, the challenge is likely to prove difficult. As *ex p. B* shows, the courts are reluctant to challenge an assessment that a treatment is ineffective, unless it can be shown that there is a clear flaw in the reasoning used.

In Charlene's case, the *Rogers* case should be referred to. It may be argued that this is too restrictive on what will count as an exceptional case (there is no reference to disabled adults who are not elderly). Article 14 of the ECHR could be used if the policy is seen to discriminate on the basis of disability.

In Dave's case, the *Rogers* decision suggests that such personal characteristics should not be relied upon. See also the NICE (2006) guidance on this.

FURTHER READING

Harris, J. (2005) 'Its not NICE to Discriminate', 31 *Journal of Medical Ethics* 373.

Herring, J. (2007)'Where are the Carers in Healthcare Law and Ethics?', 27 *Legal Studies* 51.

Maynard, A. (2001) 'Ethics and Health Care "Underfunding"', 27 *Journal of Medical Ethics* 223.

Newdick, C. (2005) *Who Shall We Treat?* Oxford University Press: Oxford.

NICE (2006) *Social Value Judgements*. London: NICE.

Syrett, K. (2002) 'NICE Work? Rationing, Review and the 'Legitimacy Problem' in the New NHS', 10 *Medical Law Review* 1.

Syrett, K. (2004) 'Impotence or Importance? Judicial Review in an Era of Explicit NHS Rationing', 67 *Modern Law Review* 289.

3

Consent to treatment

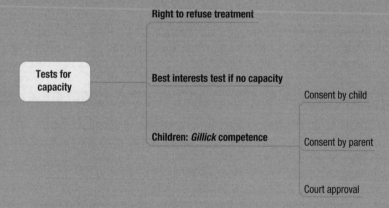

Tests for capacity
- Right to refuse treatment
- Best interests test if no capacity
- Children: *Gillick* competence
  - Consent by child
  - Consent by parent
  - Court approval

A printable version of this topic map is available from www.pearsoned.co.uk/lawexpress

Revision Checklist

What you need to know:

- [ ] How the law defines capacity
- [ ] How decisions are made for those people who lack capacity
- [ ] When it is permissible to administer medical treatment without an individual's consent
- [ ] The legal effect of 'advance decisions'

Introduction

A doctor should only provide treatment to a competent patient with that patient's consent.

This apparently simple proposition is, in fact, far more complicated than at first appears. First, there is the question of what it means for a patient to have capacity. Second, there is the question of how much information a patient must be given in order to be able to make an effective decision. Third, there is the question of how patients who lack capacity should be treated.

Essay question advice

Essay questions on this topic will require a good knowledge of the legal principles, but also the ethical ones. You will need a detailed knowledge of the Mental Capacity Act 2005 and be able to explain how the courts will assess capacity and how decisions are made on behalf of those who lack capacity. You may also be asked to discuss how seriously the law takes the rights of patients to make decisions about their treatment. Here you would need to consider not only what the courts say they are doing, but also the actual results in the cases. Some people are suspicious that the courts find a patient to lack capacity if they disagree with his or her decision. Another topical issue which could appear in an essay question is how much information a patient should be given. The notion of 'informed consent' has received much attention from the courts and academics. On the ethical principles, you will need to explain the principle of autonomy and how it is seen as such an important principle. But you need also to be able to discuss the concerns about over-emphasising autonomy and objections to the principle.

Problem question advice

A problem question is likely to require you to discuss a number of issues raised by this chapter. There may well be some debate over whether a patient lacks capacity or not. There may also be a discussion about what decision should be made if they do, indeed, lack capacity. In answering these, the Mental Capacity Act 2005 now governs the law and there is little case law discussing the new legislation. However, you can use earlier case law as a guide to indicate how the Act might be interpreted. The problem question may also raise questions about an advance decision. Note, in particular, that generally an advance decision does not need to be in writing, but it does if it involves the refusal of life-saving treatment.

Sample question

Could you answer this question? Below is a typical problem question that could arise on this topic. Guidelines on answering the question are included at the end of this chapter, whilst a sample question and guidance on tackling it can be found on the Companion Website.

Problem question

Angelina is aged 25 and has been badly injured in a car crash. Doctors wish to use a new treatment which has been developed following embryo research, without which it is very likely she will die. Angelina has been seen by a psychologist who explains that she is aware that she is very ill, but is finding it very difficult to concentrate because she is in great pain. The psychologist says that Angelina is not in a position to understand the exact nature of the treatment she is being offered, or the risks associated with it. She is, however, aware that the treatment could save her life. Angelina says that she does not want the treatment and she wants to die. Before the accident, Angelina had been completing a doctorate in medical law. The doctorate was arguing strongly against the use of medical treatments developed using embryo research. Angelina was a member of her local church and her pastor says that her church believes that people should never refuse life-saving treatment. The pastor is adamant that Angelina would have wanted the treatment. Angelina's boyfriend is also confident that she would have wanted the treatment. Angelina's mother is opposed to her being given any treatment. There is a note in Angelina's diary which says that if she is ever ill, everything should be done to save her life.

◼ The basic approach of the law

A key principle in medical law is that competent patients have the right to refuse treatment. 'Doctors know best' may or may not be true, but if a competent patient has not consented to the treatment, the doctor cannot force it on him/her. This is true, as the following case shows, even if some might regard the patient's decision as bizarre.

KEY CASE

Re C (Adult: Refusal of Treatment) [1994] 1 WLR 290

Concerning: whether a competent adult has the right to refuse treatment

Facts

C had been diagnosed as suffering from paranoid schizophrenia and was a patient at Broadmoor. One of his delusional beliefs was that he was a great doctor. He was diagnosed with gangrene in his foot. He was told he needed to have an amputation of the foot without which he would die. C accepted that that was the doctors' view but disagreed with them. In any event, he believed God would heal him. He refused to consent to treatment. The doctors sought permission to amputate the foot.

Legal principle

Thorpe J held that C was competent. He understood what the doctors were saying to him. He understood that they believed he would die without the treatment. He was able to reach the clear decision of his own to reject their opinions. Patients should not be found incompetent simply because they do not agree with medical opinion or their decision is regarded by others as irrational. The doctors were therefore not allowed to operate on him without his consent. (It later transpired that his foot made a remarkable recovery!)

The principle in this case is reflected in the Mental Capacity Act 2005.

KEY STATUTE

Mental Capacity Act 2005, section 1(3)

A person is not to be treated as unable to make a decision merely because he makes an unwise decision.

The law is clear that simply because a decision is regarded as unwise, a patient must not be found to be incompetent. But some academics have argued that, in fact ,the courts have given way in some cases to deeming a patient incompetent, because the judge believes that the decision reached is absurd (e.g. Harrington (1996)). Of course, an obvious sign that a person lacks competence is the making of absurd decisions. On the other hand, a proper respect for autonomy must give effect to mistaken decisions or else it does not mean very much. There are ethical debates to be had here too. If a person's thinking is illogical and contradicts other values which are important to him, does it actually promote his autonomy to follow his decision?

▇ What is consent?

In order for a patient to give effective consent, it is not enough just that the patient says 'yes'; it must be shown that:

▪ the patient is competent
▪ the patient is sufficiently informed
▪ the patient is not subject to coercion or undue influence
▪ the patient has reached a clear decision.

▇ Competence

The test for competence is set out in the Mental Capacity Act 2005. The starting point is that person is presumed competent unless it is shown that he/she lacks capacity. The two key provisions on capacity are as follows:

KEY STATUTE	**Mental Capacity Act 2005; sections 2(1) and 3(1)**
	'2(1) ... A person lacks capacity in relation to a matter if at the material time he is unable to make a decision for himself in relation to the matter because of an impairment of, or a disturbance in the functioning of, the mind or brain.
	3(1) For the purposes of section 2, a person is unable to make a decision for himself if he is unable –
	(a) to understand the information relevant to the decision,
	(b) to retain that information,
	(c) to use or weigh that information as part of the process of making the decision, or
	(d) to communicate his decision (whether by talking, using sign language or any other means).'

■Information

A patient will be treated as sufficiently informed to make a decision if he or she understands in broad terms the nature of the proposed treatment (*Chatterton* v. *Gerson* (1981)). A patient, therefore, can consent even if he or she has not been informed of all of the risks of an operation. However, where a person is unaware of a crucial fact about the treatment, there will not be effective consent. So, where a man gave a woman a breast examination claiming falsely to be medically qualified, it was held that she had not consented to the 'treatment' (*R* v. *Tabassum* (2000)).

■The patient must be free from undue influence

A patient can only provide an effective consent if acting free from coercion or undue influence. So if it is felt that a patient is acting under pressure from, for example, a parent, then the consent will be invalid (*Re T* (1992)). A patient may also be found to be so exhausted or in so much pain as to lack capacity (*NHS Trust* v. *T* (2004)).

■ Consent to what?

Sometimes although it is clear that the patient has consented to some medical treatment there is a dispute over which medical treatment they consented to. A court will readily accept that if there is consent to an operation, there is also consent to the procedures necessary if the operation is to go ahead (e.g. the giving of anaesthetic). However, the law is also clear that giving consent to one operation is not consent to any operation!

■ Cases of negligence

Where a doctor has failed to provide information about the risks of an operation, as well as claiming that there was no consent to the operation, another potential claim is that the doctor behaved negligently. The problem, however, is in showing what loss the patient suffered as a result of the negligence, especially if the operation was a sucess! The following cases are very useful.

KEY CASE

Sidaway v. *Bethlem RHG* [1985] 1 All ER 653

Concerning: how much information should be given to a patient

Facts

Mrs Sidaway claimed that she was not warned about the risks of an operation to relieve a trapped nerve. The operation had left her paralysed. She sued in negligence on the basis that she had not been properly given the necessary information to consent effectively to it.

Legal principle

Each of the judges in the House of Lords provided a slightly different explanation. Lord Diplock thought the case should rely on the *Bolam* test (see Chapter 5). As there was a respectable body of opinion that found it acceptable not to warn patients of the risks in an operation of this kind, the doctor could not be found to be negligent. Lords Bridge and Keith agreed with the use of the *Bolam* test, but indicated that a judge may be willing to find that even if there was a body of medical opinion saying that a risk should not be disclosed, it may well not be respectable. Lord Templeman thought that doctors were only required to reveal general risks attached to an operation if they were asked about them by a patient. Lord Scarman suggested a doctor could rightly decide that warning a patient of a risk would cause such distress to the patient that it should not be done.

***Chester* v. *Afshar* [2004] UKHL 41**

Concerning: when a doctor was liable for failing to warn of a risk

Facts

Ms Chester suffered back pain. Her consultant, Mr Afshar, recommended surgery but failed to warn her of the 1–2 per cent chance of severe nerve damage. The operation was performed properly but nerve damage resulted and she was partially paralysed. The court found that if Ms Chester had been warned of the operation, she would have eventually agreed to the operation, but at a later time, having sought further advice.

Legal principle

Ms Chester was entitled to damages. Had she been made aware of the risk, she would not have consented to have the operation at the time she did. It was true that she would have consented to the operation later and it would have carried the same risks as the operation she, in fact, had. Nevertheless, there was a sufficient causal link between the negligence of Dr Afshar and the injuries suffered by Ms Chester. In part their Lordships emphasised that doctors should warn patients of the risks that medical procedures carried. They should not be able to breach those duties, but then escape liability in tort.

■ If a competent patient does not consent, is it ever permissible to still administer treatment?

The short answer is no! But that would not be 100 per cent accurate. There are a few circumstances where it might. Under the 1988 Public Health (Infectious Diseases) Regulations, a magistrate can order a person suffering from a 'notifiable disease' (e.g. cholera) to be detained for treatment. Although the law is not completely clear, it appears that it is also lawful to use medical treatment to prevent a person from committing suicide (*R* v. *Collins and Ashworth Hospital ex p. Brady* (2000)). A more representative case of the current law would be *St George's* v. *S* (see page 5) where it was found to be unlawful to perform a Caesarean section operation on a woman who did not consent to it, even though without it she and her baby would die.

FURTHER THINKING

It is worth thinking further about the principle of autonomy. Is it right that a patient has an absolute right to refuse treatment? What if a patient had an unusual DNA which could provide a cure for cancer, should he be entitled to refuse to have a sample of his hair removed? Or what of a patient who refuses treatment and, as a result, the burden falling on his family is much greater than would otherwise be? See Bailey-Harris (2000) and Harrington (1996).

■ The treatment of incompetent adults

So, if a patient is incompetent, how are medical decisions to be made? There are two key questions. First, who makes the decision? Second, on what basis are the decisions to be made?

Who decides?

The Mental Capacity Act 2005 determines how to determine who will make the decision on behalf of an incompetent person. It is whoever is highest up the following list:

■ the patient if his/her wishes are clear in an advance decision, made while the patient had capacity;
■ a person appointed by the patient as having a lasting power of attorney;
■ the deputy appointed by the court.

If none of these exist, is it best to apply to the court for the appointment of a deputy. Failing that, a medical-health professional can treat patients in a way which best promotes their best interests. Notice that if there is an effective advance decision stating that a patient does not want to receive treatment, a doctor should not provide it.

KEY DEFINITION

Advance Decision. An advance decision is a decision made by a patient about the treatment he/she wished to receive, or not to receive, if he/she lost capacity. It must have been made when the patient was over 18 and had capacity. The advance decision only becomes effective when the patient loses capacity.

KEY STATUTE

Mental Capactiy Act 2005, section 26(1)

'If P [the patient] has made an advance decision which is –

(a) valid, and
(b) applicable to the treatment,

the decision has the effect as if he had made it, and had had capacity to make it, at the time when the question arises whether the treatment should be carried out or continued.'

REVISION NOTE

There are special rules regarding advance decisions to refuse life-saving treatment (see Chapter 9). These need to be in writing, signed and witnessed.

EXAM TIP

You must appreciate that the advance decision only applies to refusals of treatment. You cannot through an advance direction demand that you be given treatment. Although, of course, when deciding whether it would be in a patient's best interests to give a particular treatment, the fact that a patient has explicitly stated in advance to want it, will be a relevant factor. The ethics of advance directives are also complex. Is it right that individuals at one point in time can determine what treatment they will receive at a later point in time (see Dresser (1994))? Is it possible for someone to know what he or she will want when later becoming incompetent? Or do advance directives provide a way of helping people keep control of their lives, even when they lose capacity?

How are decisions to be made on behalf of an incompetent person?

This is (at first) an easy question. The answer is that the decision must be made based on what is in the best interests of the person. But that is much easier to say than to put into practice. The MCA gives some guidance on what factors may be taken into account in determining what is in a patient's best interests.

KEY STATUTE

Mental Capacity Act 2005, section 4(6)

'(a) the person's past and present wishes and feelings (and, in particular, any relevant written statement made by him when he had capacity),

(b) the beliefs and values that would be likely to influence his decision if he had capacity, and

(c) the other factors that he would be likely to consider if he were able to do so.'

Problem area: Best interests or substituted judgement?

In some jurisdictions the law uses the doctrine of **'substituted judgement'**. The decision-maker must make the decision for the incompetent person based on what he/she thinks the person would have decided if the person had been competent. This will often be the same as asking what is in their best interests, but not always. It may be, for example, that the person had a religious objection to a treatment which would be in his/her best medical interests. Note that under the Mental Capacity Act 2005, in deciding what is in a person's best interests, the courts are required to consider the beliefs of the person, but it is unclear how much weight should be given to them.

The Mental Capacity Act 2005 makes it clear that the decision must be made based on what is best for the patient who lacks capacity. The decision should not be made just because that is what is most convenient for the individual's family or those looking after him. However, it is not always easy to separate out the interests of patients and their families as the following case shows.

KEY CASE

Re Y (Mental Patient: Bone Marrow Donation) [1997] 2 FCR 172

Concerning: whether bone marrow could be taken from a patient lacking capacity

Facts

Y was severely mentally handicapped. She lived in a community home, but was regularly visited by her mother. Y's sister suffered a bone disorder. The only real chance of recovery was if bone marrow was taken from Y and given to the sister. The court was asked to authorise the harvesting of the bone marrow.

Legal principle

The procedure was lawful because it would be in Y's best interests. Y did not have a close relationship with her sister. However, if the sister were to fall more seriously ill and die, this would affect the mother's ability to visit Y and care for her. For Y it was important that her visits with her mother continued successfully. The harvesting would be only a 'minimal detriment' to Y. It was, therefore, in Y's best interests.

▉Medical treatment of children

A child is a person under the age of 18. In order to treat a child, a doctor needs effective consent. This can be provided by any of the following:

▊ a child aged 16 or 17
▊ a *Gillick* competent child
▊ a person with parental responsibility for the child
▊ an order of the court.

If the case is a medical emergency and it not possible to obtain one of these consents, then a doctor may have a defence under the doctrine of necessity.

KEY DEFINITION

A *Gillick* competent child. A child who has sufficient maturity and understanding to make a competent decision about the issue. The child will need to understand not only the medical issues involved, but also the moral and family questions.

Notice, that although a competent child can effectively consent to treatment, if the child refuses, the parents can still consent on the child's behalf. Indeed, even if the child and his or her parents refuse to consent to the treatment, the court can still authorise it. The courts have done this in cases where children and parents belong to the Jehovah's Witnesses religious group and refuse to consent to the child receiving a life-saving blood transfusion (e.g. *Re E* (1993)).

FURTHER THINKING

The current state of the law in relation to children is controversial and there is much to discuss. In effect, the courts have said that a competent child has the right to say 'yes' but not the right to say 'no'. This is because even if the child refuses treatment, unlike an adult, consent can be provided by someone else. Some commentators argue that if the child is as competent as an adult, he or she should be treated in law as an adult. Others argue that the current law is based not on protecting the rights of children, but ensuring that they receive their medical needs. Also debated are the cases where the courts have overridden the views of children and parents. Do the courts know better than parents what is good for their children? On the other hand, should parents be allowed to martyr their children? (See Bridge (2002) and Herring (2007) for a discussion of these issues.)

Chapter Summary:
Putting it all together

Answer guidelines

See the problem question at the start of the chapter.

The first issue here is to determine whether or not Angelina is competent to make a decision over her treatment. You will want to refer to the test for capacity in the Mental Capacity Act 2005. Note that it needs to be shown that she is able to understand the issues and able to reach a decision.

If she is found competent, remember that she has an absolute right to refuse treatment. Refer to the case law on this.

If she is found incompetent, you will need to determine who can make the decision on Angelina's behalf. You will need to consider whether or not there has been an advance decision in this case, based on what is in the diary. If this is ineffective, who is the nearest relative?

Whoever the decision-maker is he or she must make the decision based on what is in Angelina's best interests. Note that although the decision-maker may take into account her religious and other views, at the end of the day, it is a question about what is in her best interests. Note that if anyone disagrees with the decision-maker, the matter can be brought to court for a judge to rule on what is in her best interests.

FURTHER READING

Bailey-Harris, R. (2000) 'Patient Autonomy – A Turn in the Tide?', in M. Freeman and A. Lewis (eds) *Law and Medicine*. Oxford: OUP.

Bridge, C. (2002) 'Religion, Culture and the Body of the Child', in A. Bainham *et al.*, *Body Lore and Laws*. Oxford: Hart.

Dresser, R. (1994) 'Missing Persons: Legal Perceptions of Incompetent Patients', 46 *Rutgers Law Review* 609.

Harrington, J. (1996) 'Privileging the Medical Norm: Liberalism, Self-determination and Refusal of Treatment', 16 *Legal Studies* 348.

Herring, J. (2007) *Family Law*. Harlow: Pearson.

Lewis, P. (2002) 'Procedures that Are Against the Medical Interests of the Incompetent Person', 12 *Oxford Journal of Legal Studies* 12.

Maclean, A. (2004) 'The Doctrine of Informed Consent; Does it Exist and Has It Crossed the Atlantic?', 24 *Legal Studies* 386.

4
Confidentiality

Breach of contract

Legal basis for protecting confidential information

Equitable breach of confidence

Other legal wrong

Personal information

Circumstance of confidence

Unauthorised disclosure

No justification

A printable version of this topic map is available from www.pearsoned.co.uk/lawexpress

Revision Checklist

What you need to know:

☐ The legal basis of confidentiality
☐ When it is permissible to breach confidence
☐ The issues surrounding the confidentiality of genetic information
☐ What rights there are to access your medical records.

▮ Introduction

Sacred secrets.

That is how the Hippocratic Oath describes the information given by patients to doctors. The oath requires doctors not to reveal these secrets. The law likewise requires doctors generally to keep confidential information, well, confidential. Of course, the issue is not as straightforward as that. The law accepts that there are circumstances in which confidentiality can, indeed sometimes should, be breached. Although quite what these are is unclear. Further, there are the difficulties over what information is protected by confidentiality. Is everything one says to a doctor covered, or only medical matters?

Essay question advice

There are three major topics which are the most likely to be the subject of an essay question in the exam. The first is the source of the obligation of confidentiality. While there is widespread agreement that medical secrets should be kept confidential, the exact legal basis for this is unclear. The second is the circumstances in which it is permissible to breach confidentiality. You will need to be able to discuss the circumstances in which the law may permit such breaches, but also to consider whether these are justifiable. The third is the special issues surrounding genetic information. Here you will need to discuss to whom the genetic information belongs and whether there is a right not to know.

Problem question advice

Problem questions are likely to centre on a scenario where there is doubt over whether a piece of information is protected by medical confidentiality. You are also likely to have to discuss whether the disclosure of such information is justified in legal terms. As always, make sure that you discuss what the law is, rather than what you think the law should be. Notice that the law is rather unclear on when disclosure of confidential information is justified. There may be, therefore, no clearly right or wrong answer, and rather the examiner is wanting you to set out the arguments that could be put on either side, based on what the case law has told us.

Sample question

Could you answer this question? Below is a typical essay question that could arise on this topic. Guidelines on answering the question are included at the end of this chapter, whilst a sample problem question and guidance on tackling it can be found on the Companion Website.

Essay question

Does the law ever permit a health-care professional to disclose confidential medical information? Should it ever be permissible to disclose such information?

■The basis in law for confidentiality

Surprisingly, it is not easy to locate the legal basis for protecting confidential information. Revealing confidential information could amount to any of the following legal wrongs:

- a breach of contract
- negligence and so giving rise to a remedy in the law of tort
- an equitable wrong
- a criminal offence
- a breach of someone's human rights
- a breach of a statutory obligation
- a breach of a professional code of practice.

Of these, the basis which appears to be used the most often, and which, therefore, is the most important, is the equitable wrong. The elements of this are set out in the table below.

Elements of equitable breach of confidence	Authority
The information must be personal, private or intimate	*Campbell* v. *MGN* (2004)
The information must be imparted in circumstances which impose an obligation of confidence.	*Venables* v. *MGN* (2001)
An unauthorised person must see the information	*A-G* v. *Guardian* (1990)

The elements of the equitable wrong were considered in the following case.

KEY CASE

Campbell v. *MGN* [2004] UKHL 22

Concerning: the legal basis for protecting confidential information

Facts

Naomi Campbell (the supermodel) was photographed leaving a meeting of Narcotics Anonymous. The photograph was published by the *Daily Mirror*. Ms Campbell sued for breach of confidence.

Legal principle

Their Lordships held that Campbell's attendance at Narcotics Anonymous meetings was confidential. The protection of confidential information concerned 'the right to control the dissemination of information about one's

▶

private life and the right to the esteem and respect of other people' (Lord Hoffmann). Lord Hoffmann and Baroness Hale said that if a person would have a reasonable expectation that information would be kept confidential, it was protected by the law. Applying this to the facts of the case, the majority of their Lordships held that attendance for treatment of a drug addiction would be confidential. However, Naomi Campbell had spoken in public about her problems with drugs and so the mere fact she was receiving treatment was not protected. But she had not revealed the details about her treatment and so these were protected. Their Lordships explained that it was necessary to weigh up the right to protection of confidential information with the right of freedom of expression. Both of these rights were protected by the European Convention on Human Rights. The majority found in this case that the balance fell in favour of protecting the right of confidentiality, rather than freedom of expression. Notably the damages awarded were on the low side (£2,500). Baroness Hale's comment suggested that their Lordships had no great sympathy for either side: 'Put crudely, it is a prima donna celebrity against a celebrity-exploiting tabloid newspaper'.

EXAM TIP

A good answer will show awareness of the potential impact of the Human Rights Act. Note that Article 8 of the ECHR protects confidential information. However, remember that you cannot sue simply for a breach of an ECHR article. What, however, a court may do in deciding how to develop the law on equitable breach of confidence, is to consider what rights the parties have under the ECHR (see *Campbell* v. *MGN* where they did this). Most significantly, under Article 10 there is the important right to free speech. The courts will weigh up the public importance in the issue at hand, and the harm to the individual by publication when deciding whether the right to free speech should carry more weight than the right to protection of confidential information.

EXAM TIP

The professional disciplinary bodies (e.g. the BMA, the Nursing and Midwifery Council) have produced guidelines on confidentiality. In practice, many health-care professionals follow the guidance of their professional body and trust that in doing so they are in compliance with the law. You therefore, need, to be aware of the guidance that has been issued (see Herring (2006, pp. 154–6) for a summary of these).

■ When is disclosure of confidential information permitted?

Once it is established that the information is protected as confidential information, the next issue to consider is whether the disclosure is justified.

Consent

Fairly obviously, if the patient has consented to the disclosure, there is no breach of confidentiality. Hence, if a doctor passes on a patient's medical records to a consultant, at the patient's request, there is no breach.

Anonymous

In a controversial decision it has been held that the release of medical information in an anonymous form (e.g. with the patient's name deleted) does not breach confidentiality.

KEY CASE

R v. *Department of Health ex p. Source Informatics* [2001] QB 424

Concerning: whether anonymous information is confidential

Facts

Source Informatics Ltd was a company which sold information to drugs companies. It arranged for GPs and pharmacists to pass information to it. The information did not include the name of the patient, only the doctor's name and the drug prescribed. The Department of Health said that this breached confidentiality. Source Informatics sought a ruling that the Department of Health's guidance was incorrect.

Legal principle

The guidance was improper. As the patients' names were removed and there was no identifying information, the patients' privacy was not infringed. The doctors and pharmacists who had passed on the information could not be said to be breaching their duty of good faith.

The *Source Informatics* decision is controversial. Do you think it correct that if your medical information is rendered anonymous you really have no objection to it being distributed? What if the information was used for medical research to which you had moral objections? If it is anonymous, is it really still 'your' information? See Case (2003) for further discussion.

The proper working of the hospital

In *R* v. *Department of Health ex p. Source Informatics Ltd* (2001) Simon Brown LJ held that information passed within the NHS for legitimate purposes was justifiable. This might include information passed between NHS professionals and used for the purposes of treatment, audit or research (section 60, Health and Social Care Act 2001).

A threat of serious harm to others

As the following case shows, one justification for revealing confidential information is that to do so would avoid a threat of serious harm to others. This, for example, would cover a case where a man revealed to his doctor that he was abusing his child. In such a case, a doctor would be entitled to disclose that information to the relevant authorities.

KEY CASE

W v. *Edgell* [1990] 1 All ER 835

Concerning: when confidentiality can be breached

Facts

W had been detained in a secure mental hospital after a conviction for manslaughter of five people. A mental health review tribunal was considering whether W was safe to be released, and a report was commissioned from Dr Edgell. His report suggested that W was extremely dangerous. He wanted to show the report to the director of the hospital caring for W because he thought that the hospital did not realise how dangerous W was. W sought an order to prevent the disclosure of the report.

Legal principle

The Court of Appeal held that it was justifiable to disclose the report to the Home Office and the director of the hospital. The court held that the public interest justified the disclosure. There was real risk of significant harm to others.

EXAM TIP

A point to emphasise in an exam answer is that simply because it may be justified to make a disclosure does not mean you can disclose the information to anyone. In *W* v. *Edgell* it was found to be permissible for the doctor to disclose the report to the director of the hospital or the Home Office. It would not have been to disclose the information to a newspaper.

Problem area: The partners of HIV patients

A difficult and controversial issue is where it is discovered that a patient is HIV positive. The patient is in a long-term relationship but does not want to tell his partner. Of course, a doctor should encourage the patient to disclose his status, but what if the patient refuses? Could this be a case where breach of confidentiality is justified in the name of protecting others from serious harm? Or would doing that undermine the trust that potentially HIV patients have in their doctors?

Assisting police investigations

Rather oddly, there is only a very limited obligation on a doctor to disclose to the police that a patient has confessed to having committed a crime. They are required to disclose information (if requested to by police) if a driver is alleged to have committed a traffic offence (Road Traffic Act 1988, section 172). The BMA encourages doctors to disclose information if the offence is grave; the detection of the crime will be seriously delayed or prejudiced without the disclosure; and if the disclosure would only be used for the detection and prosecution of the alleged offender.

Press freedom

There may be cases where the disclosure of confidential information by a newspaper is justified in the name of generating public debate and press freedom. In *H (A Healthcare Worker)* v. *Associated Newspapers* (2002) the Court of Appeal held that a newspaper could inform the public that a health-care professional had tested positive for HIV and disclose his specialism. However, his name and employer could not be revealed.

■ Genetic information

Genetic information. This is medical information about your genes, including your DNA. This can reveal whether you have a genetically related illness or whether you are a carrier of one.

As a basic rule, genetic information is entitled to the same kind of protection as any other medical information. The difficulty is that genetic information about A may reveal genetic information about B. For example, informing a patient that he has a certain genetic condition may mean the patient will realise that either his mother or father has that condition. The courts are yet to discuss how the traditional approach to medical confidentiality applies in such a context (see Skene (2001)). Another troublesome issue is whether employers or insurers can require individuals to undertake genetic tests to see if they are likely to develop illnesses in the future. While such tests would be very useful to employers and insurers, they are likely to lead to a situation where people with 'bad' genetic make-ups are unable to find jobs or obtain insurance.

FURTHER THINKING

There has been some interesting work on 'the right not to know'. Imagine that a doctor has discovered that patient A has a serious terminal illness. Patient A has a brother (B) and it is likely that patient B also has the condition. Should B be told by the doctor? Might B rather not know of the risk that he has the condition, especially if there is no available treatment? On the other hand, B might well want to know so he can plan the last few years (if he has the condition) of his life. The problem is that the doctor cannot find out whether B is the kind of person who will want to know the medical truth, or would rather not. See Laurie (2002) and Andorno (2004) for a further discussion of this.

■ A right to access information

There is a right to access medical information held by a doctor. The most important rights can be found under the Data Protection Act 1998 and Access to Medical Reports Act 1998. Even there, disclosure can be not made if it would cause serious harm to the physical or mental health of the patient or someone else.

Chapter Summary:
Putting it all together

TEST YOURSELF

- ☐ Can you tick all the points from the revision checklist at the beginning of this chapter?
- ☐ Take the **end-of-chapter quiz** on the Companion Website.
- ☐ Test your knowledge of the cases below with the **revision flashcards** on the website.
- ☐ Attempt the essay question from the beginning of the chapter using the guidelines below.
- ☐ Go to the Companion Website to try out other questions.

Answer guidelines

See the essay question at the start of the chapter.

This essay question is in two parts. The first focuses on the circumstances in which it is permissible to breach medical confidence. The examiner does not want you to spend much time describing what information is protected by medical confidence, although an introductory paragraph summarising that would be useful. The focus of the first half should be going through the different circumstances in which a breach is justified. Don't forget the relevance of the Human Rights Act.

The second half of the essay is looking at whether a breach is ever justified. Note that although you might conclude that in a particular circumstance greater good will come from a breach than preservation, you will need to consider the wider ramifications that might flow if medical secrets are not strictly protected. In other words, although breach in this particular case may appear justified if the effect of such a breach is that people no longer trust their doctors, this may overall have harmful effects. It would be good to consider the special issues that are raised by genetic information.

FURTHER READING

Andorno, R. (2004) 'The Right Not to Know: An Autonomy Based Approach', 30 *Journal of Medical Ethics* 435.

Case, P. (2003) 'Confidence Matters: The Rise and Fall of Informational Autonomy in Medical Law', 11 *Medical Law Review* 208.

Herring, J. (2006) *Medical Law and Ethics.* Oxford: OUP.

Laurie, G. (2002) *Genetic Privacy*. Cambridge: Cambridge University Press.
Kottow, M. (1986) 'Medical Confidentiality: an Absolute and Intransigent Obligation',
    12 *Journal of Medical Ethics* 117.
Mikalowski, S. (2004) *Medical Confidentiality and Crime*. Oxford: OUP.
Skene, L. (2001) 'Genetic Secrets and the Family', 6 *Medical Law Review* 1.

5
Medical negligence

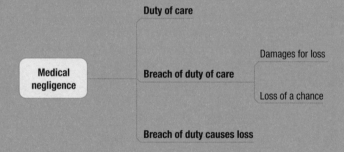

Revision Checklist

What you need to know:

☐ When a health-care professional owes a patient a duty of care
☐ How the court decides whether there has been a breach of a duty of care
☐ How damages are assessed
☐ Alternatives to the current law on medical errors.

Introduction

Doctors are meant to make you better not worse.

But occasionally things go wrong and a court may be required to decide whether a health-care professional has behaved in a negligent way and, if so, what damages are liable to be paid. The law on this area is based on the law of tort. If you have studied tort law, you should use your notes and knowledge to answer questions in this area. There are, however, difficulties in applying the law of tort in the medical context. It is not always clear what caused the injuries the victim would have suffered. There are particular problems where a doctor fails to diagnose a patient's condition. There are also public-policy concerns. If doctors are too readily found liable in negligence, there is a fear that they will engage in 'defensive medicine'. This might mean they will be over-cautious and do unnecessary tests or refuse to undertake risky surgery.

Essay question advice

There is widespread unhappiness with the law in this area and so a popular essay question will require you to consider the difficulties with the law in this area and possible reforms. You might also be asked to considered the controversial '*Bolam* test' for medical negligence. The essay is likely to ask you to analyse the meaning of the test as well as debate whether or not it is appropriate. Another issue which could arise in this area is 'loss of a chance'. This topic is one where a detailed knowledge of the case law is essential. You should also consider some of the alternatives to the system based on negligence such as the redress schemes created under the NHS Redress Act 2006 and the possibility of adopting a 'no fault' system.

Problem question advice

A problem question is likely to give rise to require you to consider a number of aspects of the law of negligence. You will need to be able to apply the '*Bolam* test'. As we shall see, there is much debate over how the *Bolam* test should be applied and whether recent cases have diluted it or not. You should pay particular attention to this debate and the cases that can be used to support either a stricter or weaker version of the *Bolam* test. You may also be required to consider how the 'loss of a chance' case law applies in a particular scenario. The recent case of *Chester* v. *Afshar* is worth knowing very well. The examiners may set a problem question which is similar to, but not identical to, the facts of that case. You will need to know why the House of Lords decided that case the way it did. There may also be issues relating to the level of damages that have to be paid, although you will not be required to provide an exact figure as to how much the court will award.

Sample question

Could you answer this question? Below is a typical problem question that could arise on this topic. Guidelines on answering the question are included at the end of this chapter, whilst a sample essay question and guidance on tackling it can be found on the Companion Website.

Problem question

Penelope is experiencing pain in her back. She is referred to a consultant, Dr House. Dr House recommends a novel form for surgery for her back pain. He fails to tell her that there is a small risk of permanent paralysis from the surgery. While performing the surgery, he sneezes and this causes an involuntary movement which causes Penelope a serious internal injury. The operation is unsuccessful and leaves her permanently paralysed. The internal injury causes her severe pain, for which there is no effective treatment. At the trial, Penelope accepts that she was in such pain that even if Dr House had informed her of the risk of paralysis, she would probably have agreed to go ahead with the surgery, although she might have sought a second opinion. Expert evidence shows that there is only a handful of experts in this field who approve of the novel form of surgery carried out by Dr House. Most think it too risky. Expert evidence also shows that any competent surgeon would be aware of the risks of sneezing and would have taken steps to ensure that it would not affect the patient. However, it was accepted that there were many reported cases of injuries caused by sneezing.

Discuss whether Penelope can sucessfully sue Dr House for negligence.

The basic principles of the law of negligence

In order to successfully bring a claim of negligence, it is necessary to show three things:

■ the professional who is being sued owed the claimant a duty of care
■ the professional breached the duty of care
■ the breach of the duty of care caused the claimant loss.

The duty of care

KEY DEFINITION

Duty of care. In the law of tort, a person owes a duty of care to all those whom that person may foreseeably harm. Occasionally, the courts hold that there are good public-policy reasons for not finding a duty of care.

There is normally little difficulty in finding that a doctor owes a patient a duty of care. This is because the basic rule is that a person owes a duty of care to anyone he or she may foreseeably injure. Of course, it is foreseeable that there is a risk of injury whenever a medical professional provides treatment to a patient. The issue can arise where a doctor comes across an injured person while going about his/her everyday business and offers no treatment. Normally, a person is not liable in tort for failing to help someone, unless there is a special relationship between them. It appears that if a doctor comes across a patient who is on his or her books, the doctor must offer assistance, but if he or she has no connection to the injured person, the doctor is free to walk on by. That was suggested in *F* v. *West Berkshire* (1989). Another issue is whether a doctor owes a duty of care to the relatives or friends of a patient (see *Goodwill* v. *BPAS* (1996) where a doctor was held to owe a duty of care to his patients, but not to those the patient would go on to have sexual relations with).

Breach of the duty of care

Normally in the law of tort, a person breaches a duty of care if he behaves in a way in which a reasonable person in his shoes would not act. However, the test in relation to medical negligence (where the claim is against a health-care professional) is slightly different. It is set out in the following case.

Bolam v. Friern Hospital Management Committee [1957] 2 All ER 118

Concerning: when a doctor is liable in negligence

Facts

John Bolam suffered a depressive illness. He was advised by a consultant to have electro-conclusive therapy. He was not told of the risk of bone fracture nor was he given relaxant drugs. He suffered several injuries. He sued the consultant in negligence.

Legal principle

McNair J held that the correct test to determine whether the consultant had behaved negligently was to ask whether he was acting 'in accordance with a practice of competent and respected medical opinion'. He went on to say, 'A doctor is not guilty of negligence if he has acted in accordance with a practice accepted as proper by a responsible body of medical men skilled in that particular art.' Here the consultant had and so he was not liable in negligence.

EXAM TIP

It is important to appreciate the significance of the *Bolam* test. It means that even though a majority of doctors would not have acted as the defendant did, if the defendant can show that a group of respected doctors would have acted in the same way, he/she can have a defence. However, note the requirement that it is a respected body of opinion. It would not be enough to point to a couple of websites which recommend the treatment!! Notice also that a doctor is judged on what the current thinking of experts was at the time when he/she acted, not what the current state of knowledge is (*Roe* v. *Minister of Health* (1954)). So, if the doctor's action was acceptable at the time he/she acted, the doctor would not be negligent, even if at the date of trial there was agreement that the action was inappropriate.

As a result of the *Bolam* test, if a doctor can show that a respected body of medical opinion would support his approach, he/she will have a defence. Part of the thinking behind this is that if doctors disagree among themselves over what treatment was best, it would not be right for a judge to decide between two competing schools of medical opinion. The judge is not in a position to determine which school of thought was better. Note also that a doctor is only expected to show the degree of skill expected of someone of his/her specialism or profession. A GP is not expected to show the same skill as a consultant specialist.

The extent to which a judge can declare a body of opinion to be not respectable is debated. In *Bolitho* v. *City and Hackney Health Authority* (1998) Lord Browne-Wilkinson appeared to suggest that if a judge decided that a particular view had no logical basis, it could be declared not logical. Some commentators (see Teff (1998)) thought this was a major shift in approach as it required the judge to subject the views of experts to some degree of scrutiny. Indeed, in *Marriott* v. *West Midlands Health Authority* (1999) although there was evidence that some doctors would approve of the way the doctor acted in not ordering further tests, their views were branded irresponsible. However, other cases have suggested it would be very rare for a judge to brand a school of medical opinion as irresponsible (see e.g. *M* v. *Blackpool Victoria Hospital* (2003)).

■ Causation

It must be shown that the negligence caused the patient's loss. So, if it could be shown that despite the negligence of the doctor no loss resulted from it, there will be no liablility to pay damages. So a doctor may be negligent in not ordering further tests, but if the further tests would not have revealed the illness of the patient, no damages will be payable. Similarly, if the doctor was negligent in failing to correctly diagnose the patient, there is no liability if even if the correct diagnosis had been made nothing could have been done to help the patient. Where it is unclear whether the cause of the patient's condition was due to negligence or some other cause, no claim in negligence can be brought (*Wilsher* v. *Essex* (1987)). It must be shown that it is more likely than not that the negligence caused the loss.

Loss of a chance cases

The most difficult cases are those where, as a result of the negligence of a health-care professional, a patient has lost a chance of being offered an effective treatment. The following are the two key legal cases:

Hotson v. *E Berkshire* [1987] AC 750

Concerning: when a claim can be brought for a 'loss of a chance'

Facts

A boy, 13, fell out of a tree. His hip was injured and he was taken to hospital. The nature and severity of his injury was not appreciated and he did not receive proper treatment. He developed a serious disability of the hip joint. The evidence suggested that if the proper treatment had been given, there would have been a 25 per cent chance that he would recover. He sued claiming that the failure to provide proper treatment had deprived him of a 25 per cent chance of an effective recovery.

Legal principle

The House of Lords rejected the approach of the trial judge who had given the boy 25 per cent of the damages he would have got if it had been shown that the medical team's negligence had caused the injury. As a general rule, their Lordships held that damages could only be awarded if it could be shown that if properly treated there would have been a greater than 50 per cent chance of recovery. So here he could not be awarded any damages.

Gregg v. *Scott* [2005] UKHL 2

Concerning: when a patient can recover damages for a lost chance

Facts

Mr Gregg consulted Dr Scott about a lump under his arm. Scott negligently diagnosed the lump as benign. It was later discovered that Gregg suffered from cancer of the lymph gland and there was a poor prognosis. The judge found that if properly diagnosed at the time, Gregg would have had a 42 per cent chance of surviving for 10 years or more, but now it was 25 per cent.

Legal principle

Mr Gregg lost his case. It had not been shown that on the balance of probabilities if he had been properly diagnosed he would have been cured. Even if properly diagnosed, the most likely scenario was that he would be in the same position that he was now. One powerful argument which influenced their Lordships was that if the claim were allowed, the impact on the NHS could be enormous.

These cases emphasise that only if it can be shown that if the defendant had not acted negligently it would be more likely than not that they would not have suffered the loss (i.e. there was at least a 50 per cent chance of being given successful treatment).

EXAM TIP

You should note that this is a controversial approach for the courts to take. Read both the dissenting as well as the majority judgments in *Gregg*. Note two objections, in particular, to the current law. First, a patient who would have a 45 per cent chance of surviving cancer but now, as a result of negligence has, only a 5 per cent chance will feel that he or she has suffered a genuine loss. Should the law not recognise this? Second, is it right that a doctor can behave negligently, but then escape liability by saying that the patient would probably be just as badly off if she/he had acted properly? Notice also the emphasis in *Gregg* v. *Scott* placed on the possible financial costs to the NHS if a patient could claim for a 'loss of a chance'. Is it fair that such an argument should play a role in developing the case law? Could not the same point be made for any sort of claim against the NHS?

Failure to warn of a risk

The leading case on this is the following:

KEY CASE

Chester v. *Afshar* [2004] UKHL 41

Concerning: when a doctor was liable for failing to warn of a risk

Facts

Ms Chester suffered back pain. Her consultant, Mr Afshar, recommended surgery but failed to warn her of the 1–2 per cent chance of severe nerve damage. The operation was performed properly but nerve damage resulted and she was partially paralysed. The court found that if Ms Chester had been warned of the operation, she would have eventually agreed to the operation, but at a later time, having sought further advice.

Legal principle

Ms Chester was entitled to damages. Had she been warned of the risk, she would not have consented to have the operation at the time she did. It was true that she would have consented to the operation later and it would have carried the same risks as the operation she had. Nevertheless, there was a sufficient causal link between the negligence of Dr Afshar and the injuries suffered by Ms Chester. Their Lordships were influenced by the importance they attached to the requirements that doctors should warn patients of the risks that medical procedures carried. They should not be able to breach those duties, but then escape liability in tort.

It is important to realise the limits of this case. Notice that it was crucial that the claimant was able to demonstrate that if she had been informed of the risks, she would have had the operation at a different time because she would have sought other advice. It seems if the evidence had shown that she would have had the operation at the same time, she would have lost the case.

Do you think the decision in *Chester* v. *Afshar* was motivated as much by a wish to punish a doctor who behaved negligently as it was to compensate the complainant for her loss? What, in fact, was her loss here? She accepts that, but for the negligence, she would have had the operation anyway, and the operation would have been as risky as the one she had. Was her real loss a lack of proper information? Notice the emphasis placed on patients' rights to be informed of risks in the majority's judgments. Some commentators suggest that a similar emphasis on patients' rights was not found in *Gregg* v. *Scott*. Do not patients also have a right to be diagnosed with reasonable skill?

Harm to secondary victims

The law of tort is generally reluctant to award damages to a person who is psychologically harmed by witnessing harm suffered by others. Therefore, where a patient is harmed by the negligence of a doctor, it is unlikely that the relatives of a patient will be able to sue for damages for the psychological distress they suffer at seeing the patient suffer. However, there is no complete bar on such a claim if a relative is actually in the room when the patient is negligently injured. Relatives may also be able to claim if their distress was directly caused by the negligence of a health-care professional. This might be where they are told in a particularly callous way that their relative has died.

◼Damages

The damages available following a successful medical negligence claim follow the same principles as general tort law. They can include expenses incurred as a result of the injuries, loss of earnings due to the injury, and compensation for pain and suffering.

◼The NHS Redress Act 2006

There has been increasing dissatisfaction with the way that the current law on medical negligence operates. Some believe litigation encourages the NHS and its staff to become antagonistic towards patients who have been injured. It might even discourage doctors from being honest when something has gone wrong, for fear that they will be sued. Certainly, the legal costs to the NHS and patients is huge. Often the legal costs exceed the costs of any damages the courts award. Some research has suggested that what patients who have been harmed by bad medical practice really want is an apology and a reassurance that a similar thing will not happen to other people, but there is no ready means of doing that apart from suing. The NHS Redress Act 2006 allows the Secretary of State to set up a more informal process by which a person with a complaint against the NHS can use a redress scheme which will not involve going to court. Where a complaint is made out, the patient may receive an apology, an explanation, a report of what will happen to ensure there will not be a repetition, and/or compensation.

EXAM TIP

You may be asked in the exam to consider the problems with the current law. In doing so, you should consider the effectiveness of schemes created under the 2006 NHS Redress Act. Some commentators have suggested that if a patient is harmed as a result of medical treatment, he or she should receive compensation whether or not there was fault on the part of doctors. They claim that this will mean there will be less stigma attaching to doctors found to have caused harm to a patient, and that might mean that they will be more open about what has happened. It is also said that it avoids the difficult the law faces in finding whether or not a doctor has been negligent. Opponents of such 'no fault' schemes argue that if a doctor has behaved negligently, it is in the public interest that this be made known.

■ The licensing of medicines

There are special rules that deal with the development and manufacture of medicines. These are governed by the Medicine Act 1968. It is likely in future that there will be European guidelines governing this area.

■ Regulation by professional or NHS bodies

As well as regulation by the courts, there are professional and NHS bodies which regulate medical professionals. These include bodies such as the General Medical Council and National Patient Safety. These can bar professionals from acting by striking them off the relevant professional register. They can also require professionals to undergo further training or bar them from acting in a particular area.

Chapter Summary:
Putting it all together

Answer guidelines

See the problem question at the start of the chapter.

There is no problem here in establishing that Dr House owes Penelope a duty of care. The question is whether he breaches the duty. Note that there are three claims here. The first is that he was negligent in the way he did the operation. The *Bolam* test would need to be applied: is there a respectable body of opinion which holds it appropriate to do surgery if you are prone to sneeze?!

The second is whether it was appropriate to do this kind of surgery at all, given that many doctors believe it too risky. Again, the *Bolam* test would need to be considered. A good answer would examine whether the subsequent case law has diluted the *Bolam* test at all.

The third (and this is harder) is the failure to warn of the risks. Here *Chester* v. *Afshar* will need to be considered. In *Chester* much weight was attached to the fact that if properly warned of the risks, the patient would not have agreed to have the operation at the time she had it.

If there is a breach, you will need to consider how the court will award damages. Notice that the damages in *Chester* v. *Afshar* appear to match the amount to cover the injury suffered.

FURTHER READING

Brazier, M. and Miola, J. (2000) 'Bye-Bye Bolam: a Medical Litigation Revolution', 8 *Medical Law Review* 85.

Davies, M. (2006) *Medical Self-Regulation*. Aldershot: Ashgate.

Harris, J. (1997) 'The Injustice of Compensation for Victims of Medical Accidents', 314 *British Medical Journal* 1821.

Merry. A. and McCall Smith, R.A. (2001) *Errors, Medicine and the Law*. Cambridge: CUP.

Teff, H. 'The Standard of Care in Medical Negligence – Moving on from *Bolam*?', 18 *Oxford Journal of Legal Studies* 473.

Lord Woolf (2000) 'Are the Courts Excessively Deferential to the Medical Profession?', 9 *Medical Law Review* 1.

6
Contraception, abortion and pregnancy

Grounds for abortion

Risk of injury to woman

Risk of grave permanent injury to woman

Risk to the life of woman

Risk of physical or mental abnormalities to fetus

The difference between abortion and contraception

Regulation of pregnancy

Right to refuse treatment

Best interests test used if competent

A printable version of this topic map is available from www.pearsoned.co.uk/lawexpress

Revision Checklist

What you need to know:

- [ ] The difference between contraception and abortion
- [ ] The circumstances in which an abortion is legal
- [ ] The circumstances in which a woman can be forced to have a Caesarean section without her consent.

Introduction

When does life begin?

This is a question which has been troubling lawyers, philosophers and politicians for centuries. Yet, it is central to the debates over abortion and pregnancy. It is easy for the debates over these issues to become polarised between those who are 'pro-life' and those who are 'pro-choice'. Pro-lifers claim that human life begins at conception or shortly thereafter. The law should therefore protect the life of the unborn child with as much rigour as it protects other human life. Pro-choicers emphasise that it should be a woman's right to choose what should happen to her body and her fetus. Most legal systems are a compromise between these views: not treating the fetus with the same rights as an adult, but neither allowing a woman to do whatever she wants with the fetus.

Essay question advice

Essay questions in this area will require you to demonstrate a good knowledge of the law as well as an awareness of the ethical debates surrounding the subjects. Be careful not to get carried away when writing your essay. You need to show a sensitivity to the complex issues that surround this subject. Even if you have strong views, you need to discuss respectfully the views of others and explain carefully why you disagree. Do not assume that the extreme 'pro-choice' or 'pro-life' views are the only ones available; there is a range of compromise positions as well which you should consider.

The two most likely areas to arise as problem questions would be abortion or enforced Caesarean section cases. In relation to abortion, you will need to have a detailed knowledge of the Abortion Act 1967 and the criminal offences which will be committed if that Act is not complied with. In relation to cases surrounding enforced Caesarean sections, you will need to separate out two key questions. First, does the woman have capacity to consent to the operation? Second, if she lacks capacity, would the operation be in her best interests? Alternatively, if she has capacity, how does the law treat a competent refusal in this context? You will need to be able to discuss some of the leading cases on the topic.

Sample question

Could you answer this question? Below is a typical problem question that could arise on this topic. Guidelines on answering the question are included at the end of this chapter, whilst a sample essay question and guidance on tackling it can be found on the Companion Website.

Problem question

Marion is a passionate believer that births should be natural and opposes medical intervention during pregnancy. While in labour she is told that a Caesarean section is mandated and without it she and the fetus will die. She is torn between her desire to give birth to a healthy baby and for a natural birth. She tells her medical team 'Don't do a Caesarean, but make sure the baby is not hurt'. The doctors sedate her and perform a Caesarean section.

Consider whether or not the doctors acted lawfully.

■Contraception

The law on contraception has had to move with the times. Recently Mumby J in *R (Smeaton)* v. *Secretary of State for Health* (2002) stated that contraception was 'no business of government, judges or the law'. In fact, section 5(1)(b) of the National Health Service Act 1977 requires the Secretary of State for Health to ensure that 'all reasonable requirements' for treatment and advice on contraceptive issues are met. The main legal issue concerning contraception is the dividing line between the provision of contraception and abortion. The provision of contraception is largely unregulated. While abortion is tightly controlled by the Abortion Act 1967, the distinction was explored in the following case.

R (Smeaton on behalf of SPUC) v. *The Secretary of State for Health et al.*
[2002] 2 FCR 193

Concerning: the definition of contraception and miscarriage

Facts

The Society of the Protection of the Unborn Child challenged the legality of a statutory instrument which permitted the sale of the 'morning after pill' without prescription. The SPUC claimed that the use of the pill caused a miscarriage or abortion and, therefore, involved criminal offences under section 58 or 59 of the Offences Against the Person Act 1861. The use of the pill would, therefore, only be lawful if the requirements of the Abortion Act 1967 were satisfied. The government argued that the pill was contraception and so was not governed by the Act and could be given without prescription.

Legal principle

Munby J rejected the view that the word 'miscarriage' meant any procedure that caused the loss of a fertilised egg. A miscarriage only occurred where there had been an established pregnancy. Munby J also held that there would be harmful social effects if emergency contraception could only be given if the requirements of the Abortion Act 1967 were met. He, therefore, held that the 'morning after pill' could be sold without prescription and that using it would not amount to an offence.

KEY DEFINITION

Contraception. A procedure or device which prevents fertilisation of the egg or the implantation of the fertilised egg.

■ Abortion

To perform an abortion without legal authority is a criminal offence. The two main offences which could be committed are:

KEY STATUTE

Offences Against the Person Act 1861, section 58

'Every woman, being with child, who, with intent to procure her own miscarriage, shall unlawfully administer to herself any poison or other noxious thing, or shall unlawfully use any instrument or other means whatsoever with the like intent and whosoever, with intent to procure the miscarriage of any woman, whether she be or not with child, shall unlawfully administer to her or cause or be taken by her any poison or other noxious thing, or shall unlawfully use any instrument or other means whatsoever with the like intent, shall be guilty of an offence . . .'

KEY STATUTE

Infant Life Preservation Act 1929, section 1

'. . . any person who, with intent to destroy the life of a child capable of being born alive, by any wilful act causes a child to die before it has an existence independent of its mother, shall be guilty of an offence.... Provided that no person shall be found guilty of an offence under this section unless it is proved that the act which caused the death of the child was not done in good faith for the purpose only of preserving the life of the mother.'

Problem area: Is there a right to an abortion?

Notice that the starting point for the law is that an abortion is a criminal offence. The Abortion Act 1967 sets out the circumstances in which doctors have a defence to what would otherwise be a crime. It is, therefore, somewhat misleading to say that the Abortion Act 1967 protects the right to have an abortion (see Fox (1998)). Indeed (as we shall see), in the legislation it is the view of the doctors, rather than the choice of the woman, which is seen as key to the legality. It might be argued that a right to an abortion can be found through the Human Rights Act 1998.

EXAM TIP

In the unlikely event of a doctor being charged with performing an unlawful abortion, he or she would probably seek to argue that the procedure was permissible under the terms of the Abortion Act 1967. In an exam it is also worth referring to the defence of necessity at common law (*R* v. *Bourne* (1939)). It is not clear when this applies, but it certainly would be available where without the procedure the woman would die or suffer a serious harm.

The Abortion Act 1967

For an abortion to be lawful, the abortion must comply with the requirements of the 1967 Abortion Act. These are set out in the table below.

Requirement for an abortion to be lawful under the Act	Source
Abortions must be carried out under the authority of a registered medical practitioner	Abortion Act 1967, s 1(1)
Abortions can only be carried out in an NHS Hospital or other approved place	Abortion Act 1967, s 1(3)
All abortions must be notified to the Department of Health	Abortion Regulations 1991
Two medical practitioners must believe that at least one of the statutory grounds permitting abortion is made out	Abortion Act 1967, s 1(1)(a–d)

The statutory grounds for abortion are as follows:

Risk of injury to the health of the woman

KEY STATUTE

Abortion Act 1967, section 1(1)(a)

The pregnancy has not exceeded its twenty-fourth week and that the continuance of the pregnancy would involve risk, greater than if the pregnancy were terminated, of injury to the physical or mental health of the pregnant woman or any existing children of her family.

Notice that you can only rely on this ground if the pregnancy has not exceeded its twenty-fourth week. It needs to be shown first that there would be a risk to the physical or mental health of the woman or any of her existing children. And second that this risk is greater if the pregnancy continued than if the pregnancy is terminated. It is unclear what an injury to mental health includes. Surely it would cover the risk of a woman suffering depression. But would it cover a risk of emotional upset? If so, this ground would be very broad indeed.

Grave permanent injury to the health of the woman

KEY STATUTE

Abortion Act 1967, section 1(1)(b)

The termination is necessary to prevent grave permanent injury to the physical or mental health of the pregnant woman.

This ground is harder to prove than section 1(1)(a). The harm involved to the woman needs to be grave, permanent, and an injury. Emotional upset would not, on its own, be sufficient to satisfy this ground. This ground can be used however far advanced the pregnancy is.

Risk to the life of the woman

KEY STATUTE

Abortion Act 1967, section 1(1)(c)

The continuance of the pregnancy would involve risk to the life of the pregnant woman, greater than if the pregnancy were terminated.

This is, perhaps, the least controversial ground for an abortion. Note that it only needs to be shown that there is a risk to the life of the woman. It does not need to be shown that this is necessarily a high risk.

Serious handicap of the child

KEY STATUTE

Abortion Act 1967, section 1(1)(d)

There is a substantial risk that if the child were born it would suffer from such physical or mental abnormalities as to be seriously handicapped.

This ground has no time limit and so can be used however far advanced the pregnancy is. There has been some debate over the words 'substantial' here and also over the word 'serious'. In 2005, a curate challenged the legality of an abortion of a fetus which had a cleft palate (see *Jepson* v. *Chief Constable of West Mercia* (2003)). That challenge failed. This suggests that the definition of a serious handicap is not too difficult to satisfy.

FURTHER THINKING

There has been some dispute over the theoretical basis for the disability ground. Is it suggesting that if a child is born seriously disabled, their life will be so appalling that it would have been better for the child not to be born? Or is the ground justified on the basis that the burden of caring for a seriously disabled child is so heavy that it should not be imposed on a reluctant parent. If the former, is this in effect a form of disability discrimination? Is the law saying that it would be better for disabled people not to be born? If it is the latter, might not the law say to a child of a disabled person that if he/she is not willing to care for the child, then the state can arrange foster care or alternative arrangements? See Scott (2005) for further discussion of this issue.

EXAM TIP

In an exam answer you should emphasise that the Abortion Act 1967 does not require that one of the four statutory grounds is, in fact, made out, but rather that two doctors were *of the opinion* that it is. In *Paton* v. *BPAS*, George Baker P suggested that only if it were shown that the doctors were acting in clear bad faith would the statutory grounds not be made out. This also emphasises that it is the doctors' views on whether the grounds exist which matters, not the woman's. Note also that under the Abortion Act 1967, section 4, if a medical professional has a conscientious objection to abortion, he/she does not have to participate in an abortion. It has been claimed that in some parts of the country this has led to difficulties accessing abortion services.

Attempts to stop abortions taking place

The courts have generally been very reluctant to make an order preventing an abortion or declaring that an abortion would be illegal. Courts have refused applications by fathers to prevent a mother having an abortion (*Paton v. BPAS* (1979)). Similarly unsuccessful have been attempts to bring proceedings 'in the name of the fetus' to prevent an abortion (*Paton v. BPAS* (1979)). Most controversially, it has been held in the following case that parents have no right to prevent their children from having abortions.

KEY CASE

R (on the application of Axon) v. *Secretary of State for Health (Family Planning Association intervening)* [2006] EWHC 37 (Admin)

Concerning: under-16-year-olds and the law on abortion

Facts

Mrs Sue Axon had two teenage daughters. She challenged official guidance issued by the Department of Health which allowed health-care professionals to offer abortion services to under-16-year-olds without consultation with the child's parents. Mrs Axon claimed the guidance was unlawful and illegitimately interfered with her human rights as a parent.

Legal principle

Silber J held that if a young person was competent to consent, then abortion services could be offered and provided to her. Although the young person should be encouraged to inform her parents, there was no obligation for the parents to consent to such treatment or even be informed of it. Silber J held that the Human Rights Act 1998 did nothing to change the legal position on this.

REVISION NOTE

In reaching the decision in *Axon*, the judge placed a lot of weight on the decision of the House of Lords in *Gillick* v. *West Norfolk and Wisbech*, discussed in Chapter 3. Although from the discussion of the law on children and consent generally, in theory at least, even if a child did not want to have an abortion, a doctor could rely on the consent of her parent in order to give her one.

■ The legal status of the fetus

The legal status of the fetus is unclear. In *Attorney-General's Reference (No. 3 of 1994)* (1998) Lord Mustill described the fetus as a 'unique organism'. In *Vo* v. *France* it was held that a fetus had no right to life under the European Convention on Human Rights, but that it would not be contrary to the Convention for a country to enact legislation protecting the fetus. The following points can be made about the English law:

Legal points about a fetus	Authority
A fetus is not a person in the eyes of the law	*Attorney-General's Reference (No. 3 of 1994)* (1998)
A fetus is not simply part of the mother	*Attorney-General's Reference (No. 3 of 1994)* (1998)
It is not possible to bring proceedings 'in the name of the fetus'	*Paton* v. *BPAS* (1979)
A fetus cannot be made a ward of the court	*Re F (In Utero)* (1988)
A fetus has interests which are protected by the law	*S* v. *St George's NHS Trust* (1998)
A fetus is not directly protected by the European Convention on Human Rights	*Vo* v. *France* (2004)

FURTHER THINKING

The ethics of abortion are controversial and complex. To some the key point is the status of the fetus. If the fetus is a person, it has a right to life and cannot be killed. If, however, it is not a person, the fetus can be removed at the wish of the woman. Feminists argue that it is impossible to consider the issue of abortion without looking at the wider social context. Restricting women's access to abortion can be seen as a means of controlling women's lives. You should be aware of the range of views available on the issue, not just the more extreme ones. The article by Thomson (1971) is interesting because it argues that, even if one believes that the fetus is a person with a right to life, it would still be improper not to permit abortions because that would be imposing too great a burden on the woman (see Finnis (1973), for a rejection of her views). Note also the discussion in Brazier (1988) which considers whether, if the issue of whether a fetus is a person is essentially a religious one and incapable of scientific assessment, the law should 'impose' that view on pregnant woman. See Herring (2006, pp. 247–65) for a summary of the ethical debates.

■ Regulation of pregnancy

Should the law restrict the way pregnant women behave in order to protect the fetus? There is scientific evidence that a fetus can be seriously harmed by a mother's and father's behaviour during the pregnancy. Should we restrict the rights of parents to, for example, smoke during a pregnancy? The law has generally been very reluctant to do so. The issue has most dramatically arisen in cases where a woman refuses to have a Caesarean section operation without which the fetus will die. In many cases (see e.g. *Re MB* (1997)) the courts have concluded that the woman is not competent, and so the operation can go ahead. Where, however, she is competent, her wishes must be respected.

KEY CASE

St George's Healthcare NHS Trust v. *S* [1998] 3 All ER 673

Concerning: whether it was lawful to perform a Caesarean section operation on a woman without her consent

Facts

S was 35 weeks pregnant when she was told she needed to have a Caesarean section operation. She was told that without one she and/or the fetus would die. She refused to consent. Her doctors assessed her competent to make the decision to refuse, but sought judicial approval to perform the operation. This was given by Hogg J and a baby girl was born as a result. After the birth, the mother appealed against Hogg J's decision.

Legal principle

The Court of Appeal held that the mother's detention and the performance of the operation without her consent was unlawful. They confirmed that a competent woman had an absolute right to refuse treatment. This was not affected by the fact that she was pregnant. This is so even if without it she and the fetus will die.

■ Chapter Summary:
■ Putting it all together

Answer guidelines

See the problem question at the start of the chapter.

The first issue to be determined is whether or not Marion is competent. See the test for capacity in the Mental Capacity Act, discussed in Chapter 2. You should note the willingness of the courts in cases of this kind to find a woman in labour incompetent (see e.g. *Re MB* (1997)). But notice the warnings in *S* v. *St George's* (1998) that the courts should not find a woman incompetent simply because they find her decision irrational.

If she lacks capacity the court will make a decision based on what is in her best interests (again, see Chapter 2). Note that in the case law (e.g. *Re MB*) it is generally assumed that it is in the best interests of a woman who is in the late stages of pregnancy to give birth.

If she has capacity, the next issue is to consider what she has decided about her treatment. Here her views appear contradictory. Note that for the doctors to perform the operation, they need her consent to the operation (a lack of objection is insufficient). Consider the arguments on either side on how best to understand the woman's views here.

FURTHER READING

Brazier, M. (1988) 'Embryos' 'Rights': Abortion and Research', in M. Freeman (ed.) *Medicine, Ethics and the Law*. London: Stevens.

Dworkin, R. (1993) *Life's Dominion*. London: Harper Collins.

Finnis, J. (1973) 'The Rights and Wrongs of Abortion', 2 *Philosophy and Public Affairs* 117.

Fox, M. (1998) 'A Woman's Right to Choose: A Feminist Critique', in J. Harris and S. Holm (eds) *The Future of Human Reproduction.* Oxford: OUP.

Herring, J. (2006) *Medical Law and Ethics.* Oxford: OUP.

Mason, K. (2005) 'What is in a Name? The Vagaries of *Vo* v. *France'*, 17 *Child and Family Law Quarterly* 97.

Scott, R. (2005) 'Interpreting the Disability Ground of the Abortion Act', 64 *Cambridge Law Journal* 388.

Thomson, J.J. (1971) 'A Defense of Abortion', 1 *Philosophy and Public Affairs* 1.

7

Reproduction

Unlawful reproductive activities

Forms of assisted reproduction

Regulated reproductive activities

Unregulated reproductive activities Who is the parent of a child?

A printable version of this topic map is available from www.pearsoned.co.uk/lawexpress

Revision Checklist

What you need to know:

☐ The variety of techniques available in assisting reproduction
☐ The ways the law regulates reproductive services
☐ Who can access reproductive services
☐ Who is the parent of a child
☐ The legal regulation of surrogacy; cloning and embryo selection.

Introduction

Producing children has never been more complicated.

True, there is there the ever popular traditional method (sexual intercourse), but there is also available a range of alternatives. The law sometimes appears to have trouble keeping up with the fast pace of change in this area. There are two major issues facing the law. The first is how to regulate the reproductive services on offer. Should all kinds of reproductive service be available? And should they be open to everyone? The second is the question of who should be regarded as the parents of a child born as a result of reproductive services.

Essay question advice

It is difficult to predict which question may be asked on this topic. There is a wide range for the examiner to choose from: access to reproductive services; issues surrounding surrogacy; embryo selection; cloning; determining parentage. All of these could be selected. However, there are some theoretical themes which run through this topic. One is the concept of reproductive autonomy. It will be very useful to be aware of this issue and the arguments for and against it. Another issue concerns the status of the embryo. The position in law appears to be that although the embryo is not a person, it is protected to some extent by the law. If then the law recognises that the embryo has some interests, what exactly are these?

Problem question advice

The most obvious area for a problem question to arise would be over the parentage of a child. You are likely to face a scenario where a number of people could claim to be the father or mother of the child. To answer such a question you will need to have a good understanding of the relevant case law and the provisions of the Human Fertilisation and Embryology Act 1990. You should note, however, that in interpreting the legislation, the courts have attempted to ensure that a 'sensible' result is reached. Also, don't forget the option of adoption. So if the people actually raising the child are not in law the parents, they could apply to adopt the child and become parents that way.

Sample question

Could you answer this question? Below is a typical problem question that could arise on this topic. Guidelines on answering the question are included at the end of this chapter, whilst a sample essay question and guidance on tackling it can be found on the Companion Website.

Problem question

Adam and Eve are an unmarried couple who have had trouble conceiving a child. They approach a licensed clinic for treatment. They are offered treatment using donated sperm, from Dave, and a donated egg from Mary. During the weeks they are receiving information and tests, Adam and Eve's relationship comes to an end. However, they do not inform the clinic of this. After the break-up Eve attends the clinic alone but reassures the staff that she is still in a relationship with Adam. She then, by chance, meets and falls in love with Dave. Dave goes along with Eve to the clinic on the day the embryo is implanted. Dave and Eve marry shortly before baby Cain is born. Who are Cain's parents?

■Some key theoretical issues

Behind many of the issues raised in this chapter is the concept of reproductive autonomy.

KEY DEFINITION
Reproductive autonomy. Supporters of reproductive autonomy argue that the decisions people make about whether or not to have children are intimate and profoundly important. The state should assist couples in their choice. Where a person or a couple wishes to have a child, the state should assist them as far as is possible (given other restraints on resources). It is not the state's job to decide whether a person will make a good or bad parent or to restrict the way a person wishes to create a child. Sometimes the concept is distinguished from 'reproductive liberty' where, while the state should not prevent someone having a child, it is not under a positive obligation to assist her/him.

Supporters of reproductive autonomy often point out that the state does nothing to prevent people from becoming parents if they are able to have a child 'naturally'. The state does not even stop a known paedophile from fathering a child (of course, it would be difficult for it to do so). So, surely the state should not prevent people who suffer infertility from becoming parents. Otherwise, the state will be discriminating on the grounds of disability (infertility). Opponents argue that while the state cannot prevent people from becoming parents 'naturally', it would be irresponsible to allow people, whose children would suffer, to become parents.

FURTHER THINKING
It is well worth getting familiar with the debates over the notion of reproductive autonomy (see Jackson (2001)). One issue which has not been addressed sufficiently by opponents of reproductive autonomy is that if we are to restrict who can have access to reproductive services, who should make the decisions: clinicians, the HFEA, judges? Also, under the current law the cost of assisted reproductive techniques prevents many people from accessing these services, is that justifiable?

■ The different techniques of assisted reproduction

The most commons forms of reproductive techniques are as follows:

Reproductive technique	What it involves
Cyrpopreservation	This involves freezing sperm or ova or embryos
Assisted insemination by partner	Here the sperm of the woman's partner is placed inside her and it fertilises one of her eggs
Donor insemination	Here sperm from a donor is used and placed inside a woman to fertilise one of her eggs
In vitro fertilisation	Here eggs are removed from a woman and fertilised in a laboratory. The fertilised egg is then returned to the woman. Sperm from a partner or a donor may be used
Intra-cytoplasmic sperm injection	A sperm (from a partner or donor) is injected into an egg (from the woman or donated). The fertilised egg is then transferred back inside the woman

The issues raised by these different techniques vary enormously. For example, where a wife simply has her husband's sperm placed inside her, this raises few, if any, legal or ethical issues. It is where the treatment involves the sperm of a donor or the creation of embryos outside the woman that the issues become more complex.

■ The regulation of the Human Fertilisation and Embryology Authority

The Human Fertilisation and Embryology Authority (HFEA) regulates much assisted reproduction through the Human Fertilisation and Embryology Act 1990 (HFEAct).

Activities which are unlawful under HFEAct

The HFEAct prohibits certain reproductive activities and does not permit the HFEA to license them. These are as follows:

Unlawful reproductive activity	Statutory provision
No embryo can be stored for more than 14 days after the mixing of the gametes	HFEAct, s 4(3)
A non-human embryo or gamete (e.g. that of an animal) cannot be placed in a woman	HFEAct, s 3(2)
It is unlawful to place a human embryo in an animal	HFEAct, s 3(3)
Eggs taken from embryos cannot be used in fertility treatment	HFEAct, s 3A
It is unlawful to alter the genetic structure of any cell which is part of an embryo	HFEAct, Sch 2, para 1(4)
It is unlawful to clone a person	Human Reproductive Cloning Act 2001

Activities only lawful if done under a licence from HFEA

There are certain activities which are illegal unless the clinic has been licensed to do them by the HFEA. These are:

Activity only lawful if licensed	Statutory provision
The storage of an embryo	HFEAct, s 41
The storage and use of gametes	HFEAct, ss 3 and 4

Activities which do not require a licence

There is, of course, no need to obtain a licence to engage in sexual intercourse! But nor is there any need to have a licence for so-called 'do-it-yourself insemination' if it involves live gametes and there is no storage involved.

■ Controversial issues involving assisted reproduction

Disputes over frozen embryos

What if a couple use their gametes to produce an embryo which is stored by a licensed clinic, but they split up and one of them wants the embryo destroyed and the other does not? That issue was dealt with in the following case which made it clear that the embryo had to be destroyed.

KEY CASE

Evans v. *Amicus Healthcare; Evans* v. *UK* **[2004] 3 All ER 1025; [2006] 1 FCR 585.**

Concerning: how to resolve disputes over frozen embryos

Facts

Natalie Evans and Howard Johnston were engaged when they underwent IVF treatment. Ms Evans was undergoing cancer treatment and they were told that they should freeze embryos because after the treatment she would be unable to have any children of her own. Six embryos were created and frozen with the intent that they would be used once Ms Evans had completed her treatment. In 2002 the couple separated and Mr Johnston asked the clinic to destroy the embryos. Ms Evans wanted to use the embryos to become pregnant. If they were destroyed, she would lose all chance of having children of her own.

Legal principle

The Court of Appeal held that under the terms of the Human Fertilisation and Embryology Act 1990 a clinic was only entitled to store an embryo if both the people who had provided the gametes which had produced the embryo consented to the embryo being stored. Once one party withdrew consent, the embryos had to be destroyed.

The Court of Appeal also held that there was nothing in the Human Rights Act 1998 which required the courts to reach a different conclusion. Ms Evans appealed ultimately to the Grand Chamber of the European Court on Human Rights. The Chamber held that the case involved a clash of Article 8 rights. Mr Johnston's right not to be a father against his wishes; and Ms Evans's right to be able to become a mother. It was up to each individual country to decide how to balance these competing rights under their 'margin of appreciation'. The choice of English law to prefer Mr Johnston's rights could not be said to be improper.

It is well worth having a good think about the issues raised in *Evans v. UK* (see Lind (2006)). Do you agree that the right not to be a parent is as important as a right to be a parent? Which would be a greater interference in how people wish to live their life: to be a parent against his/her wishes, or not being able to be a parent when he or she wishes to be? Do you think the interests of the embryos should have had any role to play in the decision?

Restrictions to treatment

When a couple approaches a clinic for treatment, the clinic must consider whether it is appropriate to offer them treatment services. This will involve the likelihood of success. More controversial is section 13(5), HFEAct.

> **KEY STATUTE**
>
> ### Human Fertilisation and Embryology Act 1990, section 13(5)
>
> A woman shall not be provided with treatment services unless account has been taken of the welfare of any child who may be born as a result of the treatment (including the need of that child for a father), and of any other child who may be affected by the birth.

Some clinics, as a result of section 13(5), have not offered (or only rarely offered) services to lesbian couples or single women, although other clinics have been willing to offer to these groups. Clinics might also consider the age of the parties seeking treatment. Is it appropriate to offer reproductive services to a woman who will be a pensioner when her child is a teenager?

Embryo selection

Some forms of reproductive assistance lead to the creation of several embryos; some of these will then be implanted into the woman. The clinic will normally test to see which embryos are healthy before deciding which to implant. This is not particularly controversial; much more controversial is whether other factors can be taken into account when deciding which embryos to implant. The leading case on this is the following:

Quintavalle (on behalf of CORE) v. *HFEA* [2005] UKHL 28

Concerning: the legality of selecting embryos for implantation

Facts

A couple had a child (Zain) who suffered a serious disability. The only hope of cure was if a sibling had stem cells which were an appropriate match. Using assisted reproductive techniques, the couple produced some embryos. They wanted to have them tested to see which (when born) could provide a suitable match for Zain. A licence was granted by the HFEA to do this. CORE (a 'pro-life pressure group) sought a judicial review of this.

Legal principle

Section 11 of the Human Fertilisation and Embryology Act 1990 allowed the HFEA to license certain activities. These included practices designed to secure that embryos are in a 'suitable condition' to be placed in a woman. Their Lordships held that suitable here could mean suitable to the woman concerned. This permitted the HFEA to grant this licence.

Surrogacy

Surrogacy. One woman (the surrogate mother) agrees to carry a child for another woman or a couple (the commissioning couple). Their intention is that shortly after birth the child will be handed over to the commissioning couple and they will raise the child.

Surrogacy is a controversial practice. The law's response to surrogacy is somewhat ambiguous. On the one hand, it is clear that a surrogacy arrangement is unenforceable.

Surrogacy Arrangements Act 1985, section 1A

No surrogacy arrangement is enforceable by or against any of the persons making it.

Where, therefore, the surrogate mother after birth decides that she wishes to keep the child, the commissioning couple cannot enforce the contract to hand the child over. However, they could seek a residence order under the Children Act 1989. The court would only be likely to grant this if it thought that the surrogate mother posed a risk to the child.

If the surrogate agreement works and the child is handed over the commissioning couple can either seek to adopt the child or seek a parental order under section 30 of the Human Fertilisation and Embryology Act 1990 (although the criteria for obtaining that are strict).

EXAM TIP

A popular question in the exam is whether or not surrogacy should be permitted or even encouraged in the law (see Jackson (2001)). The primary argument in favour is liberty: if all the individuals concerned are happy to enter into the contract, it should be respected and the state should not intervene. Opponents cite concerns for the well-being of any child (especially if the arrangement breaks down) and worries that a surrogacy contract is akin to slavery.

■Parentage

Who in law is a child's parent? The general rule is that a child's mother is the mother who gave birth to the child, while the child's father is the man whose sperm created the child. Where there is any doubt over this, DNA tests can be used to establish who the father is. However, the Human Fertilisation and Embryology Act 1990 makes some special provisions.

Mothers

KEY STATUTE

Human Fertilisation and Embryology Act 1990, section 27(1)

The woman who is carrying or has carried a child as a result of the placing in her of an embryo or sperm and eggs, and no other woman, is to be treated as the mother of the child.

This provision makes it clear that it is the woman who gives birth to the child who is the mother. This is so even if donated eggs were used.

Sperm donors

KEY STATUTE

Human Fertilisation and Embryology Act 1990, section 28(6)

'Where –

(a) the sperm of a man who has given consent as is required by paragraph 5 of Schedule 3 to this Act was used for a purpose for which such consent was required, or

(b) the sperm of a man, or any embryo the creation of which was brought about with his sperm, was used after his death,

he is not to be treated as the father of the child.'

This provision makes it clear that normally a sperm donor will not be a father of a child produced. However, this is only where the sperm is used in accordance with his consent. Also, under the HFEA (Disclosure of Information) Regulations 2004, SI 2004/1511, once a child born using donated sperm reaches the age of 18, he or she can ask for information about the donor father. For sperm donations after April 2005, this will include information revealing the identity of the donor. The new regulations have caused a reduction in the number of donors.

EXAM TIP

The issue of the anonymity of donors is a controversial one and it is worth revising the issue carefully. Consider the different human rights that could be claimed here? How important is a child's right to know their genetic origins? Is such a right enforceable if (as the evidence suggests) parents are unwilling to tell their children that they were born using donor sperm? If the sperm-donor shortage continues, should donor anonymity be restored?

Husbands and partners of women receiving assisted reproductive services

KEY STATUTE

Human Fertilisation and Embryology Act 1990, section 28(1)(2)(3)

'(1) This section applies in the case of a child who is being or has been carried by a woman as the result of the placing in her of an embryo or of sperm and eggs or her artificial insemination.

(2) If –

(a) at the time of the placing in her of the embryo or the sperm and eggs or of her insemination, the woman was a party to a marriage, and
(b) the creation of the embryo carried by her was not brought about with the sperm of the other party to the marriage

then ... the other party to the marriage shall be treated as the father of the child unless it is shown that he did not consent to the placing in her of the embryo or the sperm and eggs or to her insemination (as the case may be).

(3) If no man is treated, by virtue of subsection (2) above, as the father of the child but –

(a) the embryo or the sperm and eggs were placed in the woman, or she was artificially inseminated, in the course of treatment services provided for her and a man together by a person to whom a licence applies, and
(b) the creation of the embryo carried by her was not brought about with the sperm of that man,

then ... That man shall be treated as the father of the child.'

In short, if a woman has received treatment at a licensed clinic using donated sperm, then her husband will be treated as the father of any child born, unless he can show that he did not consent. A woman's unmarried partner can be treated as the father of any child born if they received treatment services together. The following cases have considered the interpretation of these provisions.

KEY CASE

Leeds Teaching Hospital v. *A* [2003] 1 FLR 1091

Concerning: who were the parents of a child following a mix of gametes in a hospital

Facts

Mr and Mrs A and Mr and Mrs B all attended a licensed clinic for infertility treatment. Due to a mistake, Mrs A's eggs were mixed with Mr B's sperm. The resulting embryo was placed in Mrs A and twins were born. The parties were happy for Mr and Mrs A to raise the children but the question arose as to who at law was the father of the child.

Legal principle

In the absence of any specific statutory provision to say the opposite, the genetic parents of a child were the legal parents. Mr B could not be regarded as a sperm donor and, was, therefore exempt from being a parent under section 28(6)(a). Mr A could not claim to be the father based on section 28(2) because he had not consented to his wife receiving this treatment with Mr B's sperm. This meant that the genetic parents (Mrs A and Mr B) were the parents of the child.

KEY CASE

In *Re D* [2005] UKHL 33

Concerning: who the father was of a child where a couple separated while receiving reproductive services

Facts

D and her male partner B attended a clinic as a couple seeking reproductive services. They signed the paperwork and started receiving services. Before an embryo was implanted D and B separated and D formed a relationship with S. A child was subsequently born. The question arose as to who was the father of the child.

Legal principle

Under section 28(3) if a man and a woman are receiving licensed treatment services together then he can be regarded as the father of any child born (even if he is not genetically related to the child). Their Lordships held that it needed to be shown that the couple were seeking the treatment as part of a 'joint enterprise'. However, for section 28(3) to operate, it had to be shown that they were receiving the treatment services together at the time when the

> **KEY CASE**
>
> embryo was implanted. This would require a court to look at the issue from the perspective of both the clinic (whom did they think they were offering services to?) and from the couple (did they still regard it as a joint enterprise?). In this case, they were no longer a couple and it would be a fiction to give D the label of father, given he was to play effectively no role in the child's life. The child, therefore, had no father.

Problem area: Interpreting *Re D*

The House of Lords in *Re D* made it clear that the crucial point in time for the purposes of section 28(3) was the moment of implantation of the embryo. It, however, leaves unclear from whose perspective it is to be judged whether the couple are receiving treatment services together: from that of the woman, the man or the clinic. Their Lordships appeared to indicate that all three should be considered, but there is little guidance on what to do if they disagree.

Chapter Summary:
Putting it all together

TEST YOURSELF

- [ ] Can you tick all the points from the revision checklist at the beginning of this chapter?
- [ ] Take the **end-of-chapter quiz** on the Companion Website.
- [ ] Test your knowledge of the cases below with the **revision flashcards** on the website.
- [ ] Attempt the problem question from the beginning of the chapter using the guidelines below.
- [ ] Go to the Companion Website to try out other questions.

Answer guidelines

See the problem question at the start of the chapter.

The key issues raised in this problem question are as follows:

- Is Eve the mother of the child? See section 27 HFEAct.
- Is Adam the father by virtue of section 28(3)? See *Re D (A Child)*. Note the need to

consider the question of whether they are receiving treatment services together from the point of view of the couple as well as from the point of view of the clinic.

▋ Can Dave be regarded as the father of the child? Note: as the husband of a woman who gives birth, he will be presumed to be the father. But will section 28(6) mean he is not if his paternity is challenged? If he is not, who will be?

FURTHER READING

Harris, J. and Holm, S. (2004) *The Future of Reproduction.* Oxford: OUP.

Harris J. (2005) 'No Sex Selection Please, We're British', 31 *Journal of Medical Ethics* 286.

Harris-Short, S. (2004) 'An "Identity Crisis" in the International Law of Human Rights? The Challenge of Reproductive Cloning', 11 *International Journal of Children's Rights* 333.

Horsey, K. and Biggs, H. (2006) *Human Fertilisation and Embryology.* London: UCL Press.

Jackson, E. (2001) *Regulating Reproduction.* Oxford: Hart.

Lind, C. (2006) 'Judgments of Solomon: Power, Gender and Procreation', 18 *Child and Family Law Quarterly* 576.

Scott, R. (2006) 'Choosing between Possible Lives: Legal and Ethics Issues in Pre-implantation Genetic Diagnosis', 26 *Oxford Journal of Legal Studies* 153.

8

Organ donation and ownership of body parts

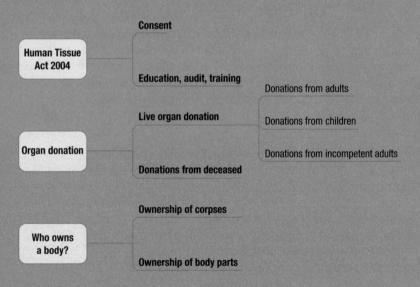

Human Tissue Act 2004
- Consent
- Education, audit, training

Organ donation
- Live organ donation
  - Donations from adults
  - Donations from children
  - Donations from incompetent adults
- Donations from deceased

Who owns a body?
- Ownership of corpses
- Ownership of body parts

A printable version of this topic map is available from www.pearsoned.co.uk/lawexpress

Revision Checklist

What you need to know:

☐ The law concerning organ donations

☐ How the Human Tissue Act 2004 regulates dealings in bodily material

☐ The way the law resolves disputes over the ownership of bodily material.

Introduction

Is your body yours?

You probably assume it is, but the law on this is far from straightforward. It is unclear whether your body is property and, if so, who owns it. And this is not just a question of interest to high-minded philosophers. Human bodies can be of huge financial value. There is a serious shortage of organs for donations. The current law is fairly strict over when a person's organs should be used for transplantation and some people believe the law should be liberalised. There is also increasing awareness of the value of an individual's DNA, especially when it can be used to develop new drug treatments. At the same time, great public outcry greeted the news that hospitals have been routinely storing parts of dead children's bodies without proper consent. This has led to a change in the law under the Human Tissue Act 2004.

Essay question advice

An essay may well ask you to consider the recently passed Human Tissue Act 2004. You need to be aware of the scandals which led to the passing of the Act. This helps explain the extensive regulation which is in place. A good answer will demonstrate an excellent knowledge of the Act. Note that the Act does not take the simple approach of saying that consent is required for any use of human tissue. You will need to consider when human tissue can be used without consent and whether these exceptions are ever justified.

Another popular topic with examiners is organ transplantation. You will need to be aware of the current law, but also the intense debates over how, if at all, the law should be reformed. A final issue which you may be asked to write about is whether the body is property and if so who owns it. A good answer will not just deal with this as an abstract legal or philosophical question but also consider specific areas where it might matter what the legal status of the body is.

Sample question

Could you answer this question? Below is a typical essay question that could arise on this topic. Guidelines on answering the question are included at the end of this chapter, whilst a sample problem question and guidance on tackling it can be found on the Companion Website.

Essay/ Problem question

To what extent are the wishes of the deceased respected in the law on organ transplantation? To what extent should they be?

■The Human Tissue Act 2004

The Act is designed to provide a detailed framework for issues relating to the taking, storage and use of human organs and tissue. However, you should realise that it does not cover all dealings with human body parts. In particular, it does not deal with:

■ The removal of materials from humans. The Act covers the use or storage of removed material but has nothing to say about when it is lawful to actually remove the material from a body.
■ The Act does not deal with eggs, sperm, or human embryos.
■ The Act only deals with the storage and use of human materials for the purposes listed in Schedule 1 of the Act (these include medical research or transplantation). They do not include, for example, the storage or taking of materials for artistic purposes or curiosity.

KEY DEFINITION

Relevant material. The HTA 2004 only covers the use and storage of 'relevant material'. This is tissue, cells and organs of human beings. It does not include sperm, eggs or embryos. Cells lines or other human material created in a laboratory are not covered.

FURTHER THINKING

The Human Tissue Act 2004 was passed following a series of scandals at hospitals (most famously at Alder Hay) where tissue and organs were removed from dead children, without the consent of the parents, and the parents were not informed of it. When what had happened was discovered, many parents were horrified. (See Price (2005) for a summary of the background to the Act). It is interesting to note that while the Act tightens up the regulation of the storage of tissue and organs, it is permissible in some circumstances to store a person's tissue without consent.

The central provision in the 2004 Human Tissue Act is section 1.

KEY STATUTE

Human Tissue Act 2004, section 1(1)

The following activities shall be lawful if done with appropriate consent –

(a) the storage of the body of a deceased person for use for a purpose specified in Schedule 1, other than anatomical examination;

(b) the use of the body of a deceased person for a purpose so specified, other than anatomical examination;

(c) the removal from the body of a deceased person, for use for a purpose specified in Schedule 1, of any relevant material of which the body consists or which it contains;

(d) the storage for use for a purpose specified in Part 1 of Schedule 1 of any relevant material which has come from a human body;

(e) the storage for use for a purpose specified in Part 2 of Schedule 1 of any relevant material which has come from the body of a deceased person;

(f) the use for a purpose specified in Part 1 of Schedule 1 of any relevant material which has come from a human body;

(g) the use for a purpose specified in Part 2 of Schedule 1 of any relevant material which has come from the body of a deceased person.

Problem area: What happens if section 1 is breached?

Although section 1 makes it clear what medical professionals must do if they are to act lawfully, the statute does not make it clear what the legal consequences are if a professional does not meet the requirements in section 1. It may be that an offence of theft will be committed or perhaps a tortious wrong.

Section 1 sets out when it is lawful to deal with certain bodily materials. It must be shown that the activity was done with the necessary consent and for a 'Schedule 1 purpose'. You need to be familiar with these terms.

Consent

If one of the activities mentioned in section 1 is done without consent, it can amount to a crime (see section 5, HTA). Whether or not there has been the necessary consent all depends on the category of person involved.

Alive adult

The normal law of consent applies (see Chapter 3). So an adult with capacity and appropriately informed can give consent to the use or storage of his/her bodily material.

Deceased adults

If the deceased has made his/her views clear these must be followed. If the person died without expressing a view about what should happen to his/her body but appointed a representative to make such decisions, then the representative's views will be followed. If there is no appointed representative then the closest 'qualifying relative' can make the decision (see section 27(4) for the list of qualifying relatives).

Children

If children are competent, they can make any decisions about the use or storage of their bodily material. If not, then a person with parental responsibility can make the decision.

Incapacitated adults

Under the Human Tissue Act 2004 (Persons who Lack Capacity to Consent and Transplants) Regulations 2006 (SI 2006/1659) there is deemed consent to store and use material from adults who lack capacity in certain circumstances. These include where the material is for use in an authorised clinical trial or where the use or storage would be in the incompetent person's best interests.

Schedule 1 purposes

Section 1 of the Human Tissue Act only renders an act lawful if you are acting for a Schedule 1 purpose. If you are not provided a statute book in the exam, you should try and remember some of the purposes in the schedule by way of example. Part 1 of Schedule 1 includes transplantation and public display; part two includes clinical audit or education and training.

■ Transplanting organs

The technological advances which have meant that an organ can be taken from one person and transplanted into another are exciting and literally life-saving for some. The legal regulation of organ donation varies between living adult donors; living child donors and deceased donors.

Living adult donors

There are no special legal problems about the donation of regenerative bodily material such as blood or bone marrow. As long as there is consent in line with the general law of consent (see Chapter 3), this is permissible. The difficulty is with donation of non-regenerative material, such as a kidney or liver.

KEY DEFINITION

Regenerative bodily material. This is bodily material which (if taken from a body) will be naturally replaced by the body. Blood or bone marrow would be good examples. Non-regenerative material will not be replaced by the body. An example would be a heart or kidney.

The law does not permit a person to donate an organ if that would cause him/her death or serious harm. Donation of a single kidney or a segment of a liver may be permissible, but not donation of a heart! The procedure must be consented to. Finally, the requirement of section 33 of the HTA must be complied with.

KEY STATUTE

Human Tissue Act 2004, section 33

'**(1)** Subject to subsections (3) and (5), a person commits an offence if –

(a) he removes any transplantable material from the body of a living person intending that the material be used for the purpose of transplantation, and
(b) when he removes the material, he knows or might reasonably be expected to know, that the person from whose body he removes the material is alive.

(2) Subject to subsection (3) and (5), a person commits an offence if –

(a) he uses for the purposes of transplantation any transplantable material which has come from the body of a living person, and
(b) when he does so, he knows, or might reasonably be expected to know, that the transplantable material has come from the body of a living person.

(3) The Secretary of State may by regulations provide that subsection (1) or (2) shall not apply in a case where –

(a) the Authority is satisfied –
  (i) that no reward has been or is to be given in contravention of section 32, and
  (ii) that such other conditions as are specified in the regulations are satisfied, and
(b) such other requirements as are specified in the regulations are complied with.'

The guidance issued by the Human Tissue Authority (2006) requires that the proposed donor be given extensive information about the procedure. Where the donor is not genetically or emotionally linked with the recipient, the donor needs to have a meeting with a clinician and an independent assessor and then the donation needs the approval of the Authority.

Children donating

There is little clear guidance on the legal position where children are donating organs. The Human Tissue Authority (2006) has stated that only very rarely will living donations from children be acceptable. If the child is not competent, it might be argued that parents cannot consent to a donation on behalf of a child except in the rare cases when such a donation will be in the interests of a child. Where the child is competent, it may well be that the child can then consent. However, it may be rare that a child would have sufficient understanding to be competent (as was suggested by Lord Donaldson in *Re W (A Minor)(Medical Treatment)* [1992] 3 WLR 758).

An incompetent adult

It is not clear whether an incompetent adult could be taken to consent. It would need to be shown that the donation was in the best interests of the incompetent person. This might be possible if the donation was to someone close to the incompetent person (see e.g. *Re Y* (1997)).

Transplants from the dead

The law regulating transplants from the dead is covered by the Human Tissue Act 2004 and the general principle. The key issue is whether there is 'appropriate consent'. As we saw above, this means first asking whether or not the deceased had made a decision about organ transplantation on death (e.g. had he signed an organ donor card?). If not, then the question is whether he has made a nominated representative and, if not, then the person who is the closest qualifying relative can make the decision.

The list of who makes the decision about donation in order of priority	Section of HTA
The deceased	s 1
The person appointed by the deceased as his/her representative	s 3
Spouse or partner	s 27
Parent or child	s 27
Brother or sister	s 27
Grandparent or grandchild	s 27
Child of brother or sister	s 27
Step-father or step-mother	s 27
Half-brother or half-sister	s 27
Friend of long standing	s 27

There has been much debate over whether or not the current law on organ donation is appropriate. Some argue that we should have an 'opt out' system. This would mean that the presumption would be that people would want to donate their organs for transplantation, unless they made it clear they did not. Under the current system, a person or that person's relatives have to positively choose that they do want to donate, if transplantation is to be lawful. Supporters of an 'opt out' system argue that it is reasonable to assume that people would want to help others. Opponents argue that you cannot do anything to a person's body without his/her consent.

■ The body as property

The question of whether we own our own bodies is not just of philosophical interest. It is of practical legal importance. The traditional approach of the law has been that the body is not property. This means that a person cannot sell his/her organs (see now Human Tissue Act 2004, section 32) which makes it an offence to deal with organs for reward. However, in more recent years, the law has been more open to the idea that in some circumstances a body might become property.

KEY CASE

R v. *Kelly* [1998] 3 All ER 741

Concerning: Whether a body is property for the law of theft

Facts

An artist and junior laboratory technician had smuggled anatomical specimens from the Royal College of Surgeons. The artist made casts from these and exhibited them at art shows. The artist and technician were prosecuted for theft of the body parts.

Legal principle

The general rule was that corpses or parts of corpses were not property. However, where corpses had 'acquired different attributes by virtue of the application of skill, such as dissection or preservation techniques, for exhibition or teaching purposes', then they could become property for the purposes of the Theft Act 1968. Therefore, the corpses in this case had become property. The Court of Appeal added that future cases might well decide that if the body parts have a 'use or significance beyond their mere existence' (e.g. for use in organ transplant), they could become property.

Problem area: When are bodies property?

It is still far from clear when bodies become property. In *Kelly* it was said that a corpse could become property if skill was applied to it. But it is unclear what this means. What if a body was washed, would that be enough? In *Moore* v. *Regents of the University of California* (1990) the American courts had to deal with a case where parts of a man's body (which contained useful genetic material) were used to develop a drug which made millions of dollars for the drug company. The question was whether the man was entitled to claim that the product was generated by him and, therefore, he was entitled to at least a share in the profits. The American courts thought not, but the issues will be before the English courts soon, too, no doubt.

Chapter Summary:
Putting it all together

TEST YOURSELF

- [ ] Can you tick all the points from the revision checklist at the beginning of this chapter?
- [ ] Take the **end-of-chapter quiz** on the Companion Website.
- [ ] Test your knowledge of the cases below with the **revision flashcards** on the website.
- [ ] Attempt the problem/essay [delete as applicable] question from the beginning of the chapter using the guidelines below.
- [ ] Go to the Companion Website to try out other questions.

Answer guidelines

See the essay question at the start of the chapter.

You will want to set out clearly when the law permits the organs of a deceased person to be used in organ transplantation. Notice that if the deceased has made it clear that he does want his organs to be used for transplantation, then his relatives have no legal basis to object. However, in practice, a doctor may decide not to use a deceased's organs if the relatives strongly object to their use.

On the ethical issue, there are some who argue that once a person has died the person has no legitimate say over what should happen to his/her body and so the person's wishes should be irrelevant. Others argue that the relatives have little claim over what happens to the body of a deceased person. Any claim they may have is weaker than that of people who need an organ transplant if they are to live (see Wilkinson (2005) for further discussion).

FURTHER READING

Chau, P.-L. and Herring, J. (2007) 'My Body, Your Body, Our Bodies', 15 *Medical Law Review* 34.

Human Tissue Authority (2006) *Code of Practice on Consent*. London: HTA.

Price, D. (2000) *Legal and Ethical Aspects of Organ Transplantation*. Cambridge: CUP.

Price, D. (2005) 'The Human Tissue Act 2004', 68 *Modern Law Review* 798.

Skeane, L. (2002) 'Proprietary Rights in Human Bodies, Body Parts and Tissue', 22 *Legal Studies* 102.

Wilkinson, T. (2005) 'Individual and Family Consent to Organ and Tissue Donation: Is the Current Position Coherent?', 31 *Journal of Medical Ethics* 587.

Wilkinson, S. (2003) *Bodies for Sale*. London: Routlege.

9
Death and dying

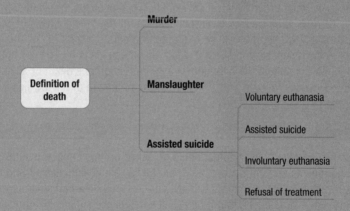

A printable version of this topic map is available from www.pearsoned.co.uk/lawexpress

Revision Checklist

What you need to know:

- [ ] The legal definition of death
- [ ] The criminal law governing murder, manslaughter and suicide
- [ ] The ethical issues surrounding euthanasia, assisted suicide and death
- [ ] The legal and ethical issues surrounding refusal of treatment
- [ ] The potential significance of the Human Rights Act 1998.

Introduction

People hold very strong views about death.

To some the law must protect the sanctity of life. To allow people to kill themselves or be killed by doctors shows a lack of proper respect for the preciousness of life. To others we must allow people to die with dignity. If a person wants to end his/her life, it is no one else's business to prevent it. After all, whose life is it? The law appears to take a strict line prohibiting the intentional causing of another's death or assistance in their suicide. However, behind this straightforward statement of the law lies a host of uncertainties.

Essay question advice

There is a wide range of essays that could be asked on this topic. It is unlikely you will get one as straightforward as 'Does the law allow euthanasia? Should it?'; it is more likely the examiners will ask you to focus on a particular aspect of the debate. For example, you might be asked whether the significance the law attaches to the distinction between acts and omissions is justified in this context; or whether the Human Rights Act 1998 should require a change in the law. Examiners will want you to be able to explain clearly what the law is, as well as discuss what you think the law should be. Made it clear in your essay whether you are discussing what the law is, or what you think it should be.

Problem question advice

Problem questions tend to focus on issues surrounding murder, manslaughter and assisted suicide. Remember to cover both the *actus reus* of the crime (e.g. did the doctor cause the death?) and the *mens rea* (e.g. did the doctor intend to kill or cause grievous bodily harm?). Unless the examiner asks you to do so in a problem question, you should be telling the examiner how the law would respond to the case, rather than discussing what you think the law should be. You may end up with the legal answer you strongly disagree with, but do not go off on a rant about it!!

Sample question

Could you answer this question? Below is a typical essay question that could arise on this topic. Guidelines on answering the question are included at the end of this chapter, whilst a sample problem question and guidance on tackling it can be found on the Companion Website.

Essay question

Does the law allow a doctor to hasten the death of a patient? Would it be justifiable for the law to be changed to permit assisted suicide but not euthanasia?

■ The definition of death

In most cases, there is no difficulty in deciding whether someone is dead or not! But in cases where a patient is in a coma or a similar state, the question becomes tricky. The issue can be of enormous practical significance in relation to organ donation. If a person's organs are available for donation, they need to be removed at an early stage; but legally they cannot be removed before a person is dead. Indeed, there has been a suspicion that some doctors wish to define death not on the basis of when a person is truly dead, but at the time which is most convenient for organ transplant. The courts have taken the view that medicine should define death. Doctors in the UK rely on brain-stem death. It is explained that when the brain-stem has died, the person ceases to have any meaningful brain activity.

FURTHER THINKING

Why does it matter when death occurs? If a person is about to die anyway, what is so very wrong in removing their organs shortly before death? Is it possible to define death or is it better to see death as a process (see Chau and Herring (2007))? Some critics of brain-stem death claim this elevates the brain to being the only organ of significance in the body. If a person's heart is still beating and their body is still working, should the fact that their brain has ceased to function be of any relevance?

■Criminal law and the ending of life

A health-care professional whose acts or omissions could cause or are connected to the death of a patient could face a number of criminal charges, most significantly:

- ■ murder
- ■ manslaughter
- ■ aiding and abetting suicide.

Murder

KEY DEFINITION

Murder. A person is guilty of murder if he or she:

- ■ caused the death of the victim
- ■ intended to cause death or grievous bodily harm
- ■ cannot successfully raise a defence.

There are two main issues which can arise in the case of a murder charge. The first is the issue of causation. Some cases have turned on whether the drugs the doctors administered killed the patient, or whether the patient died from natural causes. There can only be a murder conviction if the jury are convinced beyond reasonable doubt that the defendant caused the death of the deceased. The courts have made it clear that even if the doctor has hastened the death by a few hours, this will still amount to having caused the death of the patient (*R* v. *Arthur* (1981)). There is also some suggestion in the case law that if the doctor is providing the standard treatment for the defendant's condition, this cannot be said to cause the patient's death (see the discussion in Biggs (2001)). Although it is not quite clear what this means.

The second is the need to show intention. There are two kinds of intention recognised in the law:

- ■ Direct intention. This is where it was the defendant's purpose or aim to kill the patient.
- ■ Indirect intention. Here if the defendant realised that death or grievous bodily harm was virtually certain to result from the act, then the jury are entitled to find that there was intention (*R* v. *Woollin* (1999)).

Indirect intention is very important in medical cases. Imagine that a patient is suffering from a terminal illness and a doctor administers a pain-relieving drug which the doctor knows will hasten the death of the patient. It seems that technically this could be said to amount to indirect intention (it is not direct intention as the purpose was to relieve pain not cause death). However, it is very unlikely that a jury would decide to find that this was intention. Indeed, the jury might be directed by the judge not to find intention.

The idea of indirect intention can cause students problems. Note the following points:

(i) The law is clear that a jury may (but do not have to) find intention where death is foreseen as a virtually certainty.
(ii) If a doctor sees a patient in terrible pain and so gives the patient a lethal injection in order to end the misery, this will be a case of direct intention. This is because it is part of the doctor's aim or purpose to kill the patient. This is, therefore, subtly different from where the injection is given in order to relieve pain, although it is known that as a side-consequence the patient will die.

Cases of omission causing death

If death follows an omission by a doctor or health-care professional, a murder charge can be brought. However, there are two special points to make here:

▌ Where a patient is incompetent, a doctor must give a patient the treatment which is in the patient's best interests. However, a doctor is not required to give treatment which is not positively in the patient's best interests. Sometimes this means that even life-saving treatment need not be given.
▌ Where a patient is competent and has said that treatment may not be given, then it would be unlawful for the doctor to give the patient that treatment. This is so even where the patient is refusing life-saving treatment.

These points are illustrated by the following two cases.

KEY CASE

Airedale National Health Service Trust v. Bland [1993] AC 789

Concerning: the legality of withdrawing treatment from a patient in a persistent vegetative state

Facts

Tony Bland had been in a coma for over three years and was in a persistent vegetative state. His medical team, with the support of his family, sought authorisation from the courts to switch off his life-support machine and to cease providing nutrition and hydration.

Legal principle

The House of Lords emphasised that although Tony Bland was in a vegetative state, he was still alive. It was reasoned that withdrawing the treatment would be an omission, rather than an act. However, the omission would not breach the duty the doctors owed to him. This was because they were only required to provide treatment which was in the best interests of the patient. Giving him the treatment was not in his interests (nor was it against them).

EXAM TIP

It is important to note that *Bland* was decided before the Human Rights Act. There had been some discussion over whether the protection of the right to life in Article 2 and right to protection from torture and inhuman or degrading treatment in Article 3 could be used to reverse the *Bland* approach. However, Butler-Sloss P held that *Bland* was still good law even after the passing of the Human Rights Act (*NHS Trust A* v. *M* (2001)) because a withdrawal of treatment did not infringe Article 2.

Re B (Adult: Refusal of Medical Treatment) [2002] 2 FCR 1

Concerning: when a competent adult can refuse treatment

Facts

Ms B, aged 41, suffered paralysis from the neck down. She was dependent on a ventilator. She asked for the ventilator to be switched off, even though she knew that without it she would die. The medical team accepted that Ms B was competent, but felt unable to comply with her wishes, believing that she still had a valuable life.

Legal principle

A competent adult has an absolute right to refuse treatment. The fact that the medical team thought her decision was contrary to her best interests was irrelevant. In this case, Ms B was competent and was aware of the relevant information and knew of the alternative options. Her decision had to be respected and the ventilator switched off.

Following the Mental Capacity Act 2005 a patient can sign an 'advance decision' to refuse life sustaining treatment. Section 25 states that such a direction has to be in writing, signed and witnessed. It is not possible to use an advance decision to ask for life-shortening treatment to be given.

Manslaughter

Where the defendant did not intend to kill or cause grievous bodily harm to the patient, a manslaughter conviction may be appropriate. This is suitable where a health-care professional has killed a patient through extreme carelessness. In cases of that kind, the courts rely on 'gross negligence manslaughter'. As well as showing that the professional caused the death of the patient through a negligent act, the jury needs to be persuaded that the breach was bad enough to justify a conviction in criminal law, rather than just a liability to pay damages (*R* v. *Adomako* (1995)).

Suicide

It is not a criminal offence to commit suicide or attempt suicide. However, it is an offence to help someone else to commit suicide.

R (Pretty) v. *DPP* [2002] 1 AC 800; *Pretty* v. *UK* [2002] 2 FCR 97

Concerning: whether a person had a human right to be permitted to be killed or helped to commit suicide

Facts

Diane Pretty was suffering from motor neuron disease. She wanted the Director of Public Prosecutions to declare that if her husband helped her to commit suicide, he would not be prosecuted for assisting a suicide. The Director refused. She challenged his decision in the courts and the case went to the House of Lords and then the European Court of Human Rights. She claimed that English law in this area failed to adequately protect her human rights.

Legal principle

The House of Lords held that the law on assisted suicide was clear and the Director of Public Prosecutions had no power to issue an immunity from prosecution. As to the human rights issues, both the House of Lords and the European Court of Human Rights agreed that there was no right under the European Convention on Human Rights to be killed or to be helped to commit suicide. Indeed, the right to life under Article 2 indicated the state had an obligation to protect life.

■ Human rights and death

In *R (Pretty)* v. *DPP* and *Pretty* v. *UK* (2002) the House of Lords and ECtHR considered the potential relevance of the ECHR and made the following points:

■ Article 2: the right to life. This could not be interpreted to include a right to control the manner of your death.
■ Article 3: the right not to suffer torture or inhuman and degrading treatment. The ECtHR held that even if her medical condition amounted to inhuman or degrading treatment, it could be said that the state was inflicting that. In any event the fact that the state was required to protect the right to life under Article 2 meant that Article 3 could not be required to authorise killing.
■ Article 8: the right to respect for private and family life. The HL thought that Article 8 could not cover issues surrounding death. The ECtHR disagreed but held that even if prohibiting assisted suicide did interfere with the right of how to live one's private life, that was a justifiable interference. The state had to ensure that vulnerable people were not taken advantage of and manipulated into committing suicide. A law forbidding assisted suicide was, therefore, justifiable.

■ Article 14: the right to protection from discrimination. Mrs Pretty argued that if she was fully able-bodied, she would be able to kill herself and the law would not prevent that, but because she needed the help of a third party, the law prohibited it. This, she claimed, amounted to discrimination on the grounds of disability. The ECtHR held that if there was any discrimination, this was justified by the need to protect vulnerable people from being manipulated into committing suicide.

While most of the discussion in connection with human rights has centred on the possibility of being permitted to engage in euthanasia or assisted suicide, there have also been attempts to use human rights analysis to require doctors to provide treatment when a person is near death.

KEY CASE

R (Burke) v. *GMC* [2005] 3 FCR 169

Concerning: whether a patient can obtain an order prohibiting the withdrawal of treatment

Facts

Mr Burke suffered from cerebellar atazia. It was predicted that he would at some point in the future need to be given artificial nutrition and hydration to be kept alive. He was concerned that if he became incompetent, these might be withdrawn and he would die. He wanted an order prohibiting the withdrawal of any nutrition and hydration he required.

Legal principle

Where a patient is incompetent, the doctor must decide what treatment to provide based on what is in the patient's best interests. A patient had no right to demand a particular kind of treatment either when he is competent or incompetent. The court, therefore, refused to grant the order sought.

■ Severely disabled adults and children

Simply because the patient is a severely disabled adult or child does not change the legal position. It is still murder to do an act which causes the patient's death, with intention to cause death or grievous bodily harm. However, the disability can be relevant in a case involving an omission. As we saw earlier, in that case a doctor does not need to provide treatment that is not positively in the best interests of the patient. That is equally true where without the treatment the patient will die. In some cases, the courts have declared that if an individual is facing a quality of life which is 'intolerable', a doctor need not provide life-preserving or life-saving treatment (*Re J* (1990)). Some recent cases have not liked the language of intolerability and have preferred simply asking whether the treatment would be in the patient's best interests (e.g. *Re Charlotte Wyatt* [2005] EWCA Civ 1181). Where the doctors and the parents of a child patient disagree the matter should be brought to court (*Glass* v. *UK* (2004)).

◼ Ethical issues surrounding euthanasia

Much of the discussion of the ethical issues is confused by a failure to be clear about the terminology used:

KEY DEFINITIONS

Voluntary euthanasia. Conduct which has caused the patient's death at the patient's request.

Non-voluntary euthanasia. Conduct which causes the death of the patient without the patient's consent or objection (e.g. where the patient is in a coma and cannot consent).

Involuntary euthanasia. Conduct which kills the patient who is competent and has refused to consent to being killed.

Very few people support the idea of involuntary euthanasia. In fact, killing competent people without their consent is best described as murder. Much of the ethical dispute over euthanasia and connected issue concerns the notions of 'sanctity of life' and 'death with dignity'. Sanctity of life is the notion that life is a fundamental good. Life should be valued in itself. So even the life of a person suffering terrible disabilities should be treasured.

EXAM TIP

Keown (2002) is adamant that the principle of sanctity of life should be kept distinct from the principle of vitalism. Vitalism says that it is never justifiable to kill another person and doctors should do everything possible to keep patients alive. Keown argues that the principle of sanctity of life means it is permissible to withhold treatment which is futile (e.g. it offers no hope of benefit) or to give treatment which will hasten the patient's death if it is not intended to kill the patient (but rather, for example, provide pain relief).

Opponents of euthanasia tend to emphasise the principle of autonomy. Put simply: people should be permitted to live their lives as they wish. Doing so protects their dignity. If I decide the time has come for me to die, then that is no one else's business but my own and other people should respect my decision. Indeed, the timing of death is a particularly personal matter and so is especially deserving of respect.

FURTHER THINKING

A good understanding of the academic debates surrounding the issues of euthanasia will impress the examiners. Keown (1995) has a good collection of essays from a variety of points of view on the issue. Dworkin (1993) is a powerful case in favour of permitting euthanasia. Keown (2002) presents, with admirably clarity, the case against.

EXAM TIP

When considering the debates surrounding euthanasia and related issues it is helpful to realise there are two kinds of arguments taking place. First, there are those at the level of principle. What, based on ethical principles, would be the best position for the law to take? Second, there are those based on practical considerations. Is it possible to produce a law which allows people who wish to die, but protects vulnerable people from being taken advantage of? In this discussion, it is useful to refer to the experience of those countries which have permitted euthanasia or assisted suicide (e.g. The Netherlands; the state of Oregon in the US).

Chapter Summary:
Putting it all together

TEST YOURSELF

☐ Can you tick all the points from the revision checklist at the beginning of this chapter?

☐ Take the **end-of-chapter quiz** on the Companion Website.

☐ Test your knowledge of the cases below with the **revision flashcards** on the website.

☐ Attempt the essay question from the beginning of the chapter using the guidelines below.

☐ Go to the Companion Website to try out other questions.

Answer guidelines

See the essay question at the start of the chapter.

In this essay you need to summarise the law on this area. It is particularly important to structure your answer clearly. You will need to set out the law of murder as it applies in this context. Draw particular attention to the distinction between an act and an omission. Remember that in relation to omissions it is permissible for a doctor to withdraw treatment if that treatment is not in the patient's best interests. You will also need to emphasise the significance of intention in this context. A doctor may be permitted to administer treatment to a patient which will hasten the patient's death, if doing so is not the doctor's primary aim. You also need to emphasise that a competent patient has the right to refuse treatment, but not to demand it.

You are also asked whether it is logical to permit assisted suicide but not euthanasia. The argument in favour of such an approach is that with assisted suicide cases we can be confident that the individuals want to die (or can we?) because they have to administer the lethal substance to themselves. While with euthanasia there is a risk that although people might say they want to be killed, they may in fact not wish that. The arguments against would concentrate on those who are unable to kill themselves through disability. Is it fair that they are discriminated against by not permitting them to make the decision?

FURTHER READING

Biggs, H. (2001) *Euthanasia, Death with Dignity and the Law.* Oxford: Hart.

Chau, P.-L. and Herring, J. (2007) 'The Meaning of Death', in Brooks-Gordan *et al. Death Rites and Rights.* Oxford: Hart.

Dworkin, R. (1993) *Life's Dominion.* London: Harper Collins.

George, K. (2007) 'A Woman's Choice? The Gendered Risks of Voluntary Euthanasia and Physician-Assisted Suicide', 15 *Medical Law Review* 1.

Keown, J. (ed.) (1995) *Euthanasia Examined.* Cambridge: Cambridge University Press.

Keown, J. (1997) 'Restoring Moral and Intellectual Shape to the Law after Bland', 113 *Law Quarterly Review* 481.

Keown, J. (2002) *Euthanasia, Ethics and Public Policy.* Cambridge: Cambridge University Press.

McGee, A. (2005) 'Finding a Way through the Ethical and Legal Maze of Withdrawal of Medical Treatment and Euthanasia', 13 *Medical Law Review* 357.

10
Mental health law

Detention under Mental Health Act 1983

- Detention under section 2
- Detention under section 3 — Release from detention — Reform of the law
- Admission under section 4
- Informal treatment

A printable version of this topic map is available from www.pearsoned.co.uk/lawexpress

Revision Checklist

What you need to know:

- [ ] When a person can be detained under the Mental Health Act 1983
- [ ] How the law protects the rights of those detained under the Mental Health Act 1983
- [ ] The reforms of the law in the Mental Health Act 2007.

Introduction

The Mental Health Act 2007 has reformed the law on mental illness.

Although there was widespread agreement that the law needed to be changed, it has taken over five years to do so. This reflects how controversial the topic is. Finding the correct balance between protecting the public from people who are regarded as potentially dangerous, and protecting the rights of mentally ill people, has proved difficult. The current law permits the detention of people who, although competent, suffer from a mental illness and pose a risk to themselves or others. There is much disagreement over when it is appropriate to do this. If someone has committed no offence, is it justifiable to detain a person simply because they are thought dangerous? But if a person is known to be dangerous and is left in the community, does this fail to protect the rights of any person subsequently attacked by him or her? Further, there is the issue of how a person detained under the Act should be treated and what rights they have.

Essay question advice

Essay questions on this topic are likely to cover one or both of two issues. The first is when it is permissible to detain individuals under the Mental Health Act 1983 as amended by the 2007 Act. The second is how a person who is detained should be treated. You may also be required to discuss the recent reforms of the law. You will need to consider how the new Act has changed the law and whether it has struck the correct balance between protecting the mentally ill and protecting the public. As well as considering the details of the law, you will also need to consider the theoretical issues that arise. In particular, how the Human Rights Act impacts on mental health law and the debates over the justification for detaining competent mentally ill people.

Problem question advice

Problem questions are likely to raise issues both relating to detention and treatment of mentally ill people. You will need to have a good knowledge of the different ways that a person can be detained under the Mental Health Act 1983, as amended by the 2007 Act, and be able to explain the different grounds that need to be shown to justify detention. A good answer will be able to discuss how a human rights challenge might be made in relation to some of the grounds. You will also need to be able to explain when a person can be discharged from detention under the 1983 Act.

Sample question

Could you answer this question? Below is a typical essay question that could arise on this topic. Guidelines on answering the question are included at the end of this chapter, whilst a sample problem question and guidance on tackling it can be found on the Companion Website.

Essay question

Does the current mental health law adequately protect the human rights of mentally ill people?

■ Who is covered by the Act?

The 2007 Mental Health Act has amended the 1983 Mental Health Act to mean that only those who suffer a mental disorder are covered by the legislation. If there are concerns about someone who does not suffer a mental disorder then the Act cannot be used to assess or detain them.

KEY DEFINITION

Mental disorder is defined as 'any disorder or disability of the mind' (section 1(2), Mental Health Act 1983, as amended by the 2007 Act). The Act also refers to two things that are not mental disorders: learning disabilities and dependence on drugs or alcohol.

KEY STATUTE

Mental Health Act 1983, section 2(2)

'An application for assessment may be made in respect of a patient on the grounds that –

(a) he is suffering from mental disorder of a nature or degree which warrants the detention of the patient in a hospital for assessment (or for assessment followed by medical treatment) for at least a limited period; and

(b) he ought to be so detained in the interests of his own health or safety or with a view to the protection of other persons.'

KEY CASE

MH v. *Secretary of State for Health* [2005] UKHL 60

Concerning: whether section 2 of the MHA is compatible with human rights

Facts

M was a severely mentally disabled woman and was detained under section 2 of the Mental Health Act 1983. Under section 2 the burden lay on her to apply to the Mental Health Review Tribunal to review her detention. As M was incapable of doing this and there was a delay while her mother's application to be appointed a guardian was heard, on M's behalf it was claimed that the way section 2 placed the burden on her to bring to case before the tribunal interfered with her rights under Article 5 of the ECHR.

Legal principle

The House of Lords held that section 2, MHA was compatible with the ECHR. Article 5 did not require that every detention be subject to judicial approval. The system under the MHA gave patients and relatives easy access to the tribunal. Although a nearest relative had no right to apply to the tribunal directly where that caused problems, there were means available to ensure that the tribunal heard the case.

EXAM TIP

Note that section 2 can be used where the detention is necessary in order to protect the patient, as well as where the risk is to other people. So a suicidal patient could be detained under this provision. Although note that a person can only be detained for a maximum of 28 days.

■ Detention and treatment under section 3

This is the ground to be used if longer term detention is required. An application can only be made by an approved social worker or the patient's nearest relative.

> **KEY STATUTE**
>
> ## Mental Health Act, section 3(2)
>
> 'An application for admission for treatment may be made in respect of a patient on the grounds that –
>
> (a) he is suffering from a mental disorder of a nature or degree which makes it appropriate for him to receive medical treatment in a hospital; and
> (b) it is necessary for the health or safety of the patient or for the protection of other persons that he should receive such treatment and it cannot be provided unless he is detained under this section; and
> (c) appropriate medical treatment is available for him.'

It should be noticed that section 3 is only available in relation to patients suffering a mental disorder of the kind mentioned. It is not sufficient just to show that the individual is a danger to himself or others. Detention under section 3 is initially for six months and can be extended a further six months. Once detention is justified under section 3 yearly extensions are possible. A person can be detained under section 3 for the rest of his or her life. Continued detention requires a responsible medical officer to produce a report that indicates that the patient still suffers from a mental disorder and that treatment is necessary to prevent deterioration or alleviate the condition, or that the patient will not be able to care for themselves outside the hospital setting. The detention must be necessary for the health or safety of the patient or others. It is possible to challenge continued detention under section 3 by applying to a Mental Health Tribunal.

EXAM TIP

An issue which is well worth revising carefully is the requirement in section 3 that the condition be one where treatment must be able to improve or at least prevent the worsening of the condition if the person suffers from a psychopathic disorder or mental impairment. This means (controversially) that a person with a severe mental illness, who cannot be offered a treatment, cannot be detained. The argument in favour of this is that otherwise doctors would be keeping patients in hospitals they could offer no treatment to, but were, in effect, just incarcerating. The argument against is that it means that people who pose a danger to the public can be detained even though they have not harmed anyone.

■ Admission under section 4

Section 4 is for use in emergencies. Only a doctor can authorise admission under section 4 where the case of an urgent necessity and that waiting for a second doctor's opinion (in order to admit under section 2) would cause undesirable delay. The maximum length that a person can be detained under section 4 is 72 hours. The idea is that when the section 4 order expires, either the patient is free to go home or section 2 or 3 would be used.

■ Treatment of patients

If a patient who has been detained is competent, he or she can consent to treatment and the normal rules apply. If, however, they are competent and refuse treatment then if they have been detained under the Mental Health Act, they can be given treatment for mental disorders but not other physical conditions. The distinction between treatment for physical conditions and others is problematic.

Distinction drawn	Case
Forced feeding of someone suffering anorexia nervosa was permissible	*Re KB (Adult)* (1994)
An urgent Caesarean section on a schizophrenic woman, whose mental condition it was found would worsen if the baby died, was permissible	*Tameside and Glossop AST* v. *CH* (1996)
Treatment of a mental disorder which was not the disorder for which the person had been detained was permissible	*R (B)* v. *Ashworth Hospital* (2005)

REVISION NOTE

Remember the issue is less complex where a person has lost their mental capacity. In that case, the person can be treated under the provisions of the Mental Capacity Act 2005 and given any treatment which is in his/her best interests (see Chapter 3).

■Informal treatment

The 2007 Mental Health Act has inserted a new section 64 into the Mental Health Act 1983. This is to deal with cases where a patient is not being formally detained under the Act but is not resistant to receiving treatment for mental disorder. The treatment can be given if the patient is competent and consents, but also if the patient lacks capacity. The Act permits this if the five conditions in section 64(d) are met.

Mental Health Act 1983, section 64(d)

(1) The first condition is that, before giving the treatment, the person takes reasonable steps to establish whether the patient lacks capacity to consent to the treatment.

(2) The second condition is that, when giving the treatment, he reasonably believes that the patient lacks capacity to consent to it.

(3) The third condition is that –

(a) he has no reason to believe that the patient objects to being given the treatment; or

(b) he does have reason to believe that the patient so objects, but it is not necessary to use force against the patient in order to give the treatment.

(4) The fourth condition is that –

(a) he is the person in charge of the treatment and an approved clinician; or

(b) the treatment is given under the direction of that clinician.

(5) The fifth condition is that giving the treatment does not conflict with –

(a) an advance decision which he is satisfied is valid and applicable; or

(b) a decision made by a donee, deputy or the Court of Protection.

Problem area: The use of necessity

Prior to section 64(d), the courts had relied on the common law principle of necessity. As the European Court of Human Rights (*HL* v. *UK* (2004)) noted, the law on the treatment of those treated on the basis of necessity was unclear. One of the aims of the new Mental Health Act is to clarify the circumstances in which treatment can be given for a mental condition where the person lacks capacity, but is not being detained.

Codes of Practice

The Mental Health Act 2007 has amended the 1983 Mental Health Act to authorise the Secretary of State for Health to issue a Code of Practice. This Code of Practice is likely to become very influential in the way the law is applied. The Act sets down some principles which the Code should reflect.

KEY STATUTE

Mental Health Act 1983, section 118(2)(b)

In preparing the statement of principles the Secretary of State shall, in particular, ensure that each of the following matters is addressed –

(a) respect for patients' past and present wishes and feelings;
(b) respect for diversity generally including, in particular, diversity of religion, culture and sexual orientation (within the meaning of section 35 of the Equality Act 2006);
(c) minimising restrictions on liberty;
(d) involvement of patients in planning, developing and delivering care and treatment approriate to them;
(e) avoidance of unlawful discrimination;
(f) effectiveness of treatment;
(g) views of carers and other interested parties;
(h) patient wellbeing and safety; and
(i) public safety.

◼ The Mental Health Act 2007

The progress of the Mental Health Act 2007 through Parliament has been painfully slow. It has been the subject of fierce debates and frequent changes. In the end, the extent of reform is much less than expected. The Act does little more than make some fairly minor changes to the 1983 Act. It may well be that the Code that is to be produced under the Act turns out to be far more influential than the Act itself.

The main changes in the Act are as follows. It provides a single definition of mental disorder which will apply through all the legislation. The issue which has raised the most controversy is whether a person can be detained under the Act even if no medical treatment is available for their mental disorder. The Act makes it clear that, under section 3, a person can only be detained if there is 'appropriate medical treatment' for them. In other words, if a person is recognised as dangerous, but no treatment is available, they cannot be detained under the Mental Health Act 1983, as amended. The significance of this is lessened by the amendement by the 2007 Act of the definition of treatment in section 145 of the 1983 Act. This now includes 'specialist mental health care'. It might be thought that anyone could benefit from 'care', and so if doctors believe a person poses a genuine risk to the public, they can be detained if 'care' can be offered. The Act contains a host of other minor amendments, including, most notably, the power to make community treatment orders.

EXAM TIP

The issue which has so troubled Parliamentarians discussing the Mental Health Act 2007 is a difficult one. Is it permissible to detain a person suffering from a mental disorder who cannot be offered any treatment? In other words, is it appropriate that a person be detained simply to protect 'the public'. Doctors complain that if they detain a person they cannot treat, they are acting more like a prison than a hospital. On the other hand, if a person is known to be dangerous should they be free to live among the public? In considering this issue, you should notice that doctors have found it extremely difficult to predict correctly who, if released, might injure someone else. See Bartlett (2003) and Fennell (2005) for a full discussion of these issues.

▌ Chapter Summary:
▌ Putting it all together

TEST YOURSELF

- ☐ Can you tick all the points from the revision checklist at the beginning of this chapter?
- ☐ Take the **end-of-chapter quiz** on the Companion Website.
- ☐ Test your knowledge of the cases below with the **revision flashcards** on the website.
- ☐ Attempt the essay question from the beginning of the chapter using the guidelines below.
- ☐ Go to the Companion Website to try out other questions.

Answer guidelines

See the essay question at the start of the chapter.

A good place to start in answering the question is to set out the main human rights issues that are raised in mental health law. These include the circumstances in which a person may be detained, the reasons for which a person may be detained, the treatment to be given to a person detained under the Act, the legal position of those voluntarily receiving mental health treatment. Note that the ECHR requires there to be effective procedures to ensure that people can challenge their detention. In discussing these issues you will particularly want to address the rights under Article 3 to protection from inhuman or degrading treatment and the right to respect for private or family life under Article 8. You will then need to look at the current law and discuss the extent to which the rights you have discussed are protected.

FURTHER READING

Bartlett, P. (2003) 'The Test of Compulsion in Mental Health Law: Capacity, Therapeutic Benefit and Dangerousness as Possible Criteria', 11 *Medical Law Review* 326.

Bartlett, P. and Sandland, R. (2003) *Mental Health Law: Policy and Practice*. Oxford: OUP.

Davidson, L. (2002) 'Human Rights versus Public Detention: English Mental Health Law in Crisis?', 25 *International Journal of Law and Psychiatry* 491.

Fennell, P. (2005) 'Convention Compliance, Public Safety and the Social Inclusion of Mentally Disordered People', 32 *Journal of Law and Society* 90.

Richardson, G. (2002) 'Autonomy, Guardianship and Mental Disorder: One Problem, Two Solutions', 65 *Modern Law Review* 702.

11
Medical research

Medical research

Criminal law

Tort law
- Research involving children
- Research involving people lacking capacity
- Experimental research
- Harmful research

Ethics Committees

A printable version of this topic map is available from www.pearsoned.co.uk/lawexpress

Revision Checklist

What you need to know:

- [ ] What forms of medical research are outlawed
- [ ] When children and incapacitated adults can be involved in medical research
- [ ] How medical research is regulated

Introduction

Volunteering to take part in medical research can be risky.

In 2006, six volunteers were left seriously ill after a trial for a new drug went wrong. On the other hand, testing drugs on humans is essential if medical knowledge is to progress. The difficulties for the law is in where to draw the lines. What kinds of risks should volunteers be able to consent to? And what about children and incapacitated adults: can they be involved in medical research? The difficulty for the law has been finding a form of regulation which adequately protects the interests of participants, but does not unduly hamper medical research.

Essay question advice

Essays questions on this topic tend to focus on the legal regulation of health-care research. You will need to have a good understanding of the formal legal restrictions as well as the work of the ethics committees. You might also be asked to discuss when and whether incompetent adults or children should be involved in research. You should be aware not only of the concerns that medical research is insufficiently regulated, but also the concerns of researchers that their work is hampered by too many 'ethical' constraints.

Problem question advice

This is not a particularly popular topic for a problem question. You might be asked about a case involving an incompetent person, or a volunteer for research which is particularly risky.

Sample question

Could you answer this question? Below is a typical problem essay question that could arise on this topic. Guidelines on answering the question are included at the end of this chapter, whilst a sample problem question and guidance on tackling it can be found on the Companion Website.

ESSAY QUESTION

Are there any good reasons why medical research should be subject to any special form of legal regulation apart from the normal rules of the law of tort and crime?

■Medical research

The only kinds of medical research which are regulated are those which involve one of the following:

- ■ humans subjects
- ■ human sperm or eggs
- ■ human embryos
- ■ animals
- ■ data relating to individuals.

So research on just chemicals or bits of donated tissue are not regulated. When discussing this topic, it is important to draw a distinction between therapeutic and non-therapeutic research.

KEY DEFINITION

Therapeutic and non therapeutic. A use of a drug will be therapeutic if it is given to a patient to provide treatment for a condition from which they will suffer. This is true even if a doctor is still conducting research on the effectiveness of the drug. Non-therapeutic use would be where the doctor expects no benefits to the patient to whom the treatment is given, but is giving them the treatment simply to record its side effects or for other general research purposes.

EXAM TIP

The World Medical Association has produced the Declaration of Helsinki. This is not technically binding in English law, but is highly influential. Practitioners will regard themselves as bound by it and where the law is unclear, courts are likely to refer to it. You should, therefore, know about it and be able to make reference to it in the exam. Its cardinal principle is that 'In medical research on human

▶

subjects, considerations related to the well-being of the human subjects should take precedence over the interests of science and society' (para 5). The Declaration also emphasises the importance of having the consents of all subjects of research and the protection of the right of a subject to withdraw from any research project.

■ Regulation of research

General law

Of course, the criminal law must be complied with when conducting medical experiments. Giving a person a substance or touching them without their consent would be an offence, such an assault or battery. Similarly, the law of tort applies and so if as a result of a researcher's negligence a person suffers an injury then the researcher could be liable to pay compensation. There are also general statutes that can affect medical researchers, such as the Data Protection Act 1998 and Human Tissue Act 2004.

The consent of the participants is normally essential (although see below in relation to children and incompetent adults). It is important that research participants are given sufficient information about the research to be able to consent.

REVISION NOTE

See Chapter 3 for a discussion on the law regarding consent. Particularly relevant in this context is that the participant must be informed of any significant risks if her consent to participate in the research is to be legally effective. One difficulty in practice is that research can be severely hampered if participants leave a project mid-way through. On the other hand, the principle of consent stipulates that the participants cannot be forced to receive treatment against their wishes. Although researchers might like to bind participants to be involved in the research until the end of the project, there is no legal way of doing this.

Research which is unlawful

Research which harms the participants

Research will not be permitted if it will endanger the lives of the subjects or cause them serious harm. The difficulty is in stating how much harm is permitted. No doubt the importance of the research will play a role. Research into finding a cure for cancer may be able to justify giving trial drugs to subjects which can cause nausea. It is unlikely that research into hair loss could justify a similar level of harm. It may also be relevant if the treatment being tested will have therapeutic benefits for the subjects.

Simms v. Simms [2003] 1 All ER 669

Concerning: when experimental surgery was lawful

Facts

Two teenagers were suffering from variant Creutzfeldt-Jakob Disease. Their doctors proposed a novel treatment which had not been tested on humans. The expert evidence suggested that the effectiveness of the surgery was unknown. Without the treatment the individuals would die. Their parents sought a declaration that it was lawful for the proposed treatment to be given.

Legal principle

Butler Sloss P authorised the surgery. As the two teenagers were incompetent to make the decision, the question was simply whether doing the surgery would be in their best interests. She held that it was. Although medical opinion was divided on whether or not the treatment should be given, the experts agreed it would not be irresponsible to give the treatment. The chance of success might be slight, but given they were facing death, it was a risk worth taking. She attached 'considerable weight' to the fact the parents supported using the treatment.

FURTHER THINKING

One issue it is well worth revising is whether there is a moral duty to participate in research (see Harris (2005) and Shapsay and Pimple (2007)). If you conclude that there is a moral duty to be involved in research, do you think this is stronger or weaker if the research relates to an illness from which you suffer? Whether or not there is a moral duty to be involved in research could it affect your response to whether the law should allow children or incapacitated adults to be involved?

Research involving children

This is a controversial subject. If the child is *Gillick* competent (see Chapter 3 for a discussion of this term) then probably they can consent to being a subject of research (although Lord Donaldson in *Re W* (1992) doubted this). If the child is not competent, the child's parents may be able to consent, but parents when making decisions for children are meant to make their decisions for the benefit of the child and if the treatment is non-therapeutic that may be questioned. Despite the uncertainty over the legality of research involving treatment, it clearly happens and needs to if children are to receive effective medication.

Problem area: Is research in children's best interests?

This is a tricky issue. If parents are meant to make decisions which are in the best interests of their child, is it permissible to consent to involve your child in a research project which might cause a small amount of discomfort but not directly benefit the child? You might say that it is in children's interests to grow up realising the benefits of helping other people. The difficulty is that if children are not involved in medical research, children as a group will be harmed because it cannot be assumed that medicine which is found to be safe for adults will also be safe for children.

Research involving incompetent adults

The law on research involving incompetent adults is set out in sections 30 to 34 of the Mental Capacity Act 2005. Notably, the Act only deals with intrusive research. So if the research does not involve touching or administering a substance (e.g. it just involved watching the subject), then the special regulations in the Act do not apply. If the treatment is intrusive, then the Act lists a long list of requirements, which you should know for the exam. The most important of these are as follows

Requirement for research on incompetent person (P)	Statute
The research must be related to a condition P suffers from	MCA, s 31(1)
The research must either benefit P or be intended to assist people suffering from the same condition as P and the risk to P is negligible and the research not be unduly invasive	MCA, s 31(5)
Nothing must be done to which P appears to object, unless that is necessary to protect P from harm	MCA, s 33(2)
The research must be approved by an 'appropriate body' (e.g. the local ethics committee)	MCA, s 30

The work of research ethics committees

All large-scale medical research must be approved by a research ethics committee. Although the committee will consider the legality of any research, it is, in theory, still open to a court to decide if the research was illegal. The committee will consider the likely validity of any research, whether participants will be caused any undue pain or discomfort; that the arrangements to ensure proper information is given and consent obtained. The National Patient Safety Authority now oversees the work of ethics committees and it would be useful to visit their website (www.npsa.nhs.uk) to see the work it does and more information and what factors committees should be taken into account.

Chapter Summary:
Putting it all together

☐ Can you tick all the points from the revision checklist at the beginning of this chapter?

☐ Take the **end-of-chapter quiz** on the Companion Website.

☐ Test your knowledge of the cases below with the **revision flashcards** on the website.

☐ Attempt the essay question from the beginning of the chapter using the guidelines below.

☐ Go to the Companion Website to try out other questions.

Answer guidelines

See the essay question at the start of the chapter.

You should start this essay be explaining the ways in which the law regulates medical research. In particular pointing out that although the normal rules under criminal and tort law apply there are additional regulations. In particular discuss the work of the research ethics committees.

You will also need to consider why there is a need for special regulation. Note that historically there have been terrible abuses of people in the name of medical research (see Plomer (2005, ch. 1)).

FURTHER READING

Foster, C. (2001) *The Ethics of Medical Research on Humans.* Cambridge: CUP.

Fox, M. (1998) 'Research Bodies: Feminist Perspectives on Clinical Research' in S. Sheldon and M. Thomson (eds) *Feminist Perspectives in Health Care Law.* London; Cavendish.

Harris, J. (2005) 'Scientific Research is a Moral Duty' 31 *Journal of Medical Ethics* 291.

Plomer, A. (2005) *The Law and Ethics of Medical Research.* London: Cavendish.

Shapsay, S. and Pimple, K. (2007) 'Participation in Biomedical Research is an Imperfect Moral Duty: a Response to John Harris' 33 *Journal of Medical Ethics* 414.

And finally, before the exam . . .

By this stage you should be well advanced with your revision. If you have worked through this book and used it to provide a structure for your revision notes, you will be on course to do well in the exams.

A few final words of advice. Remember to use the case law as much as possible. This will make sure you convince the examiner that you know the law as well as being able to discuss the theory. It will also mean that when you are talking about more theoretical points they will be grounded in real practical examples and not become too 'airy fairy'.

Remember also the limitations of the law. Law works through using rules. These are used to ensure consistent decisions are made and to provide guidance for professionals and others. This means that sometimes the law cannot work in as nuanced a way as some ethicists would like. Sometimes the law will sacrifice producing the ideal result in every case, in order to produce a clear rule which will work well in the vast majority of cases.

A final point is that medical law is meant to be interesting and excite strong reactions. In essay questions you should make it clear what you think the law should be and what the ethically correct approach is. However, make sure you are able to describe a variety of different views. If they are views you disagree with, explain what you see as their main weaknesses.

TEST YOURSELF

☐ Look at the summary checklist of the points below. Are you happy that you can now tick them all? If not, go back to the particular chapter and work through the material again. If you are still struggling, **seek help** from your tutor.

☐ Go to the Companion Website and revisit the interactive **quizzes** provided for each chapter.

▶

☐ Make sure you can recall the **legal principles** of the key cases and statutes which you have revised.

☐ Go to the Companion Website and test your knowledge of cases and terms with the **revision flashcards.**

Summary checklist

Can you now:

■ Explain some of the main ethical approaches to medical issues?
■ Discuss how rationing decisions are made in the NHS?
■ Define mental capacity?
■ State how decisions are to be made for those who lack capacity?
■ Describe what medical information is protected by confidentiality?
■ Tell the examiner when a medical professional will be found liable in the tort of negligence?
■ Set out the circumstances in which an abortion is lawful and discuss the ethical issues raised?
■ Analyse the legal regulation of assisted reproduction?
■ Outline the law's regulation of organ donation?
■ Provide some guidance on whether we own our bodies?
■ Write an essay setting out the legal and ethical issues surrounding euthanasia and assisted suicide?
■ Examine when the law permits a person to be detained due to mental ill health?
■ Give a summary of how the law regulates medical research?

Glossary of terms

The glossary is divided into two parts: **key definitions** and **other useful terms**.

The **key definitions** can be found within relevant chapters as well as at the end of the book. These are the essential terms that you must know and understand in order to prepare for an examination or a piece of coursework.

The **other useful terms** provide definitions of other terms and phrases which you will encounter in this subject and may have forgotten the meaning of. These terms are highlighted in the text as they occur but the definition can only be found here.

Key definitions

Advance decision
An advance decision is a decision by a patient made about the treatment he/she wished to receive, or not to receive, if he/she lost capacity. It must have been made when the patient was over 18 and had capacity. The advance decision only becomes effective when the patient loses capacity

Consequentialism
This approach decides whether an act is ethically right or wrong by looking at its consequences. Quite simply, if it produces more good than bad, the act is ethically right

Contraception
A procedure or device which prevents fertilisation of the egg or the implantation of the fertilised egg

Deontology
This approach says that it is right or wrong to infringe certain principles, regardless of the consequences. For example, some people believe it is never right to intentionally kill another person, however much good may be produced as a result

Duty of care
In the law of tort, a person owes a duty of care to all those whom that person may foreseeably harm. Occasionally the courts hold that there are good public policy reasons for not finding a duty of care

Ethic of care
This is an ethical approach which emphasises that we all live in relationship with other people and are dependent upon other people. It, therefore, is not possible to look at a patient

	and ask what rights he or she has as a lone individual or what is best for him or her. Rather we need to ask what is best for this group of people who are in relationship together. It values interdependency and mutuality over individual freedom
Genetic information	This is medical information about your genes, including your DNA. This can reveal whether you have a genetically related illness or whether you are a carrier of one
Gillick competent child	A child who has sufficient maturity and understanding to make a competent decision about the issue. The child will need to understand not only the medical issues involved, but also the moral and family questions
Involuntary euthanasia	Conduct which kills the patient who is competent and has refused to consent to being killed
Mental disorder	'Any disorder or disability of the mind' (section 1(2) MHA 1983, as amended by the 2007 Act). The MHA refers to two things that are not mental disorders: learning disabilities and dependence on drugs or alcohol.
Murder	A person is guilty of murder if he or she: ■ caused the death of the victim ■ intended to cause death or grievous bodily harm ■ cannot successfully raise a defence
Non-voluntary euthanasia	Conduct which causes the death of the patient without the patient's consent or objection (e.g. where the patient is in a coma and cannot consent)
Principle of beneficence	Medical professionals must provide the best medical treatment for their patients
Principle of justice	Patients should be treated equally and fairly. One patient should not be improperly given preferential treatment over others
Principle of non-malfeasance	Medical professionals should not cause harm to their patients
Quality adjusted life year	This is an assessment of the benefit of a treatment. It takes into account how many years extra life a treatment may provide and the increase in quality of life that a treatment may provide
Rationing	Where there is only a limited health-care resource and a decision must be made to offer the resources to some patients and not others
Regenerative bodily material	This is body material which (if taken from a body) will be naturally replaced by the body. Blood or bone marrow would be good examples. Non-regenerative material will not be replaced by the body. An example would be a heart or kidney

Relevant material	The HTA 2004 only covers the use and storage of 'relevant material'. This is tissue, cells and organs of human beings. It does not include sperm, eggs or embryos. Cells lines or other human material created in a laboratory are not covered
Reproductive autonomy	Supporters of reproductive autonomy argue that the decisions people make about whether or not to have children are intimate and profoundly important. The state should assist couples in their choice. Where a person or a couple wishes to have a child, the state should assist them as far as is possible (given other restraints on resources). It is not the state's job to decide whether a person will make a good or bad parent or to restrict the way a person wishes to create a child. Sometimes the concept is distinguished from 'reproductive liberty' where, while the state should not prevent someone having a child, it is not under a positive obligation to assist her/him
Right	The concept of a right in law is much disputed and it is not possible to give a definition which would be accepted by everyone. When a person has a right to x, other people are bound by a duty to protect or promote the interests the person has in x. There need to be good reasons why the person should be prevented from x
Surrogacy	One woman (the surrogate mother) agrees to carry a child for another woman or a couple (the commissioning couple). Their intention is that shortly after birth the child will be handed over to the commissioning couple and they will raise the child
Therapeutic and non-therapeutic	A use of a drug will be therapeutic if it is given to a patient to provide treatment for a condition from which they will suffer. This is true even if a doctor is still conducting research on the effectiveness of the drug. Non-therapeutic use would be where the doctor expects no benefits to the patient to whom the treatment is given, but is giving them the treatment simply to record its side effects or for other general research purposes
Voluntary euthanasia	Conduct which has caused the patient's death at the patient's request

Other terms

Actus reus The part of the definition of a crime that refers to the conduct of the defendant

Mens rea The part of the definition of a crime that refers to the mental state of the defendant

Index

human tissue 90, 91
  medical research 124
torture 8
treatment *see also* consent to
      treatment, **rationing**,
      refusal of treatment
  autonomy 4–5
  demand treatment, right to
      4–5
  detention for treatment 115,
      116–20

life-saving treatment 17–18,
      32, 102–3, 108
  mental health 115–20
  necessity 118
  withholding life-saving
      treatment 17–18,
      102–3, 108

undue influence, consent to
      treatment and 28

virtue ethics 9

vitalism, principle of 108
volunteers for medical research,
      risks to 122

warnings
  consent to treatment 28,
      29–30, 50, 55–6
  medical negligence 50, 55–6
withholding treatment 17–18,
      102–3, 108